Connect

Lorraine E Murray

Copyright Lorraine E Murray 2014

Published by Connected Kids Ltd.

*The slow trickle of meditation ideas and mindfulness practices have been like drops of water. It doesn't always feel like much... but when you have a good look, you notice the bucket is already half full.*

Annabel, mother of Megan (aged 7)

*After the airplane meditation... my son asked me if meditation was magic, because his anger had just evaporated!*

Renee, mother of Jaden (aged 9)

# Connected Kids

## Help kids with special needs (and autism) **shine** with mindful, heartfelt activities

Lorraine E. Murray

Connected Kids Ltd

Dedicated to all children and young people with special needs; especially those on the autistic spectrum.

Thank you for being our greatest teachers.

**An important note:**

*Lorraine E. Murray is not a medical practitioner. The ideas in this book are based on her experience of working with children. They may complement, but should never replace, the advice and treatment of a medical specialist. If you are concerned about your child's health, please consult a medical practitioner.*

First published in 2014 by Connected Kids Ltd

© 2014 Lorraine Murray

Lorraine Murray has asserted her right under the Copyright, Designs and Patent Act 1988 to be identified as the Author of this work.

ISBN number 978-0-9931221-0-1

# CONTENTS

## Opening Karakia

*Manaakitia mai matou*
*(bless us all)*

*I tenei hui*
*(at this meeting)*

*Kei whakaro matou*
*(our thoughts are)*

*Mo te kaupapa*
*(for the rights)*

*O nga tamariki rangatahi'*
*(of children and young people)*

Tangata whenua, Lower Hutt, Aotearoa New Zealand, 2013

# FOREWORD

*"Educating children for the 21st century is a challenge. Technology is fast changing the way we live our lives. How do we prepare children for careers that haven't yet been invented? How do we help them to embrace change as an opportunity rather than as an obstacle?*

*Academic excellence is of course something all good schools strive for, but is it enough? Nurturing children's innate ability to listen in and trust their inner wisdom is a life skill that will help them find balance, peace and happiness in our competitive and changing world.*

*Lorraine Murray has played an important role in helping our school fulfil an intention that started over five years ago, as a tiny seed called yoga. Children loved the feeling of peace and calm the practice gave, especially during relaxation. This included our most active pupils, and significantly those with ADHD (Attention Deficit Hyperactivity Disorder), found quiet peace and calm that lasted beyond the confines of the yoga room. This encouraged me to maximise this experience for our children, and this led me to Connected Kids.*

*We have worked for over three years developing sessions based on the 'Connected Kids' programme. Members of staff are trained to create heart-felt meditations for our pupils. 'Quiet Time' is well established in the school providing moments of calm reflection which the children look forward to.*

*Our school is generally a calmer place now that children are learning mindful skills. This helps them now and in the future as they face the challenges and stressful demands of life. Our original seed has developed strong roots and will continue to grow and flourish as our children mature.*

*I give heartfelt thanks to Lorraine who opened the door to a plethora of possibilities that help pave the way to the peaceful lifestyle all our children deserve; a life of inner calm and confidence, peace and happiness within our exciting, demanding and innovative world."*

Christine Curtis-Perez, Primary Head Teacher
Certified Children's Yoga Teacher
Connected Kids Trainer

7

# HELLO

## ...and welcome!

You are a wonderful person for simply reading this book and I thank you. Not only will it change your life, but it will change (for the better) the lives of children when you teach them how to meditate.

My purpose in life is to teach and write about how we can give children mindful activities that bring them peace. I am particularly passionate about taking this into the lives of children with special needs. If you have any doubts that they can do this, then I have some news for you. Yes, they can.

This book was based on an experiment, to see if children with special needs could learn meditation. These children (and many since) continue to teach me time and time again that they can do this. When we trust the process, in return, they teach us that we must open our hearts to their energy. When we do, it brings peace into this world in the most profound way.

All children with autism teach us that to be in their presence we must be mindful and centred. In doing so, they show us how to be at peace in the midst of chaos. This is one of the most beautiful gifts they share with us.

Learning to teach kids with special needs is an amazing journey. I look forward to sharing this journey with you and helping you open your heart to how incredible you, and your children, truly are.

Namaste

Lorraine E. Murray

## A short (but important) introduction...

When someone wants to teach children/young people how to meditate, I ask them 2 questions;

- Do you personally practise meditation?

- Do you know *why* you want to teach children meditation?

Meditation offers many physical, emotional and mental health benefits, so this is as valuable to you as it is to children; it's a journey that brings you balance, healing and personal insights. Teaching children meditation is more than teaching them new skills, it is about showing you how to embrace a deep, heart centred connection with your kids. However it is not a way to heal or fix your child's behaviour.

If you take the time to teach your children meditation while recognising how they teach you, you will connect to them in a way that helps both of you to shine; mentally, creatively, physically, emotionally and spiritually.

## Is this book for you?

'Connected Kids' is both the name of this book and our worldwide teaching programme. Its aim is to show parents, carers and professionals how to support children with special needs using mindful activities. It will help you develop these meditation tools for your children's needs, and explain how they work from a physical, emotional, mental and energetic perspective.

The seed for this book was planted when someone asked me how to teach meditation to a child with special needs. I had touched on this in my first book 'Calm Kids - help kids relax with mindful activities', but I wanted to explore this in more depth.

During my professional practice, I witnessed positive results with kids who were on the autistic spectrum and decided to broaden my research by connecting with families and professionals worldwide who took part in case studies. This book is the result of this research; some children were on the autistic spectrum, some had ADHD (Attention Deficit Hyperactivity Disorder), anxiety issues, OCD (Obsessive Compulsive Disorder) or other special needs.

## What is a 'connected kid'?

We feel safe when we feel connected to life; to our breath, to our body, to the ground and to each other. When our children feel connected, safe and centred they can engage with life and all its joys and challenges; they can self-regulate their stress, reduce anxiety, learn more easily, develop emotional intelligence and process difficult experiences in a more peaceful way.

My intention is that this book helps you guide your children to feel that sense of connection through mindful activities; feel calmer and happier with themselves and the world at large. If you show your children how to do this, you give them an invaluable life skill to cope with life's challenges, whatever their needs.

## Centering thought for your personal meditation practice

Why do I want to teach children meditation?

*At the end of each chapter I've included a question for self-reflection during your own meditation practice. While meditating, simply focus on the centering thought. Move it from your mind to your heart centre. Breathe in the words and notice your thoughts and feelings.*

# PART ONE - preparing to teach meditation

*"By wanting to be the best mum I could, I had to learn to walk my own talk. There's no point in telling your kids how good something is for them, including meditation and then not doing it yourself. My kids have taught me that I have to begin with me in any changes I want to see."*

*Linsey Denham, Connected Kids Tutor*

To teach meditation, we have to let go of this idea that we are in control of the outcome. If we don't, we never realise what our children are teaching us.

To help us realise, we develop our own mindful practice so we can witness our thoughts and emotions; this is essential when teaching meditation. It helps us become more present with children, letting our meditations connect to children, unhindered by our expectations of how they should respond. We trust our intuition to develop the most healing, peaceful mindful activities that our kids need.

The following chapters are designed to help you to do this; to become an amazing, mindful, meditation teacher.

# 1. CONNECTING TO YOUR 'MINDFUL TEACHER'

*"Don't let the noise of others' opinions drown out your own inner voice."*

*Steve Jobs, Co-founder of Apple Inc.*

In this demanding world, being a parent or educator is an enormous responsibility. It is also a journey in personal and spiritual development.

## Mindful parenting

Being a parent presents you with the opportunity to love unconditionally. It teaches you how to let go and surrender to a bigger perspective on the meaning of life. You can come to know yourself in every sense of the word - physically, emotionally, mentally and spiritually.

For parents it can be difficult to embrace the full beauty of bringing up a child. You are often your own harshest critic, judging how good or bad your parenting skills are. You may feel overwhelmed through lack of sleep, the responsibility of caring and unsure whether to accept advice or to trust your own intuition. Parenting can also present issues that connect to your own childhood experiences - good or bad.

Mindfulness has a large part to play in helping all adults learn from their experiences with children; even the challenging ones. Mindfulness connects to your own intuition (what I call your 'mindful teacher' within) that becomes your guiding force when faced with difficult decisions.

Mindfulness doesn't mean having a quiet mind, empty of negative thoughts; it is about being present with our thoughts and feelings in the moment that we experience them. Learning to do this helps us realise how our perception influences the experience we are having.

An exhausted mother snaps and shouts at her child because of his behaviour. This is followed by feelings of guilt. Mindfulness helps this parent to release these strong emotions more peacefully as she acknowledges the stress that she's been under. With mindful practise she would be more present at the time of the challenging incident. It could help her respond differently.

Occasionally someone attends the 'Connected Kids' programme and expects a magic wand that they can wave over their children so that they behave! The reality is that I begin by teaching the adult how to be mindful. In class, we practise a mindful technique I call 'self-awareness'. This is essential for teaching children meditation, but as illustrated above, it can also help in other life experiences.

If you are not yet meditating, then please start right now, before you do anything else. Not only will it give you some useful skills to help cope with the stress of parenting, but it will set a positive example to your children and teenagers.

Try this short meditation which will help you practise some self awareness; I call it the 'mindful check in'.

## 'Mindful check-in' meditation (self-awareness)

*Whatever you are doing just take a moment to notice your breath (your eyes can be open with a soft gaze, or closed).*

*Do this by taking your attention to the tip of your nose. Now move your attention down to your chest.*

*Notice the rise and fall of your chest - pay attention to this for about 5 breaths (count them if this helps). Encourage each 'out breath' to become a little bit longer.*

*Take your attention into your body.*

*Which parts of it feel tense? Does it feel tired?*

*Using your imagination, breathe into any part of your body that feels tired or tense.*

*Listen to your body as you do this (for approx 5 breaths).*

*If your body feels uncomfortable, what can you do to change that? Does changing your position or letting go help?*

*Allow yourself to do this as you breathe out.*

*Check in with your feelings - how would you describe them in one word?*

*When you think about that feeling - where do you feel it in your body? If you aren't sure, just guess.*

*Take your attention to that part of you and just breathe in and out with the words "I am feeling (fill in the word)". Do this for about 3 breaths.*

*Repeat for another 3 breaths, but now add the words "and it's okay to feel this".*

*Watch what happens to your body, the word and your feelings after you do this.*

*Take your attention to your thoughts.*

*For 30 seconds just watch your mind - notice what it thinks about.*

*For 3 breaths, as your breathe in, silently repeat the words "I give my mind permission to relax".*

*Feel what happens in your body, feelings and thoughts when you do this.*

*Repeat this a few times if you wish.*

*Whatever the outcome, smile to yourself after you've completed your first 'check in'.*

Repeat throughout the day by just noticing a breath every now and then and checking in with your body (whatever you are doing and whoever you are with).

## Your child is your teacher

As we become more mindful we start to see the world through our children's eyes.

Your child has a tantrum. He's stressed and unhappy but doesn't have the words to articulate how he feels and this creates more frustration. It could be the environment which is overstimulating. It could be the effect of the sugar or other toxins in his diet. It could be something that happened yesterday and which has been building up over time. It could be because his body and hormones are going through enormous change as he has a growth spurt.

You can either react to this tantrum or use your mindfulness skills to help him out of the tantrum by tuning into his needs. Through this you learn how to develop tolerance and patience, or how to communicate clearly and set boundaries.

Following an 'incident', there could be a shared experience for both parent and child to reflect on challenging thoughts and feelings that came up. We need to rethink the idea of a 'naughty step' found in parenting books and consider a 'mindful moment'.

Your child teaches you how to be a parent. When he is learning to walk, you will help him take his first step. Eventually you will let him try by himself. Through this, he can learn to pick himself up after a fall and try again. As he does so, the muscles in his legs will become stronger and the corresponding neural pathways in his brain will be established. This can only happen as a result of repeated actions, and your own inner awareness that you have to trust the process.

Children with special needs, especially those on the autistic spectrum, are wonderful teachers. If we are stressed or off-balance, children with autism sense this 'energy' and reflect this back at us through their own stressed behaviours. It can be challenging, but it means we can't pretend that everything is okay. Through this, we bring ourselves back to our centre through mindfulness.

## Mindful education

As an educator, professional training and experience gives you an objective view of child development. You work with many children simultaneously and have the pressure of timetables and professional protocols.

However you are a human being, with emotions and thoughts that influence your perception of the world. Unless you are mindfully aware of this, you won't notice how your perception influences these experiences; your response to challenges will be automatic rather than mindful.

The teachers I have spoken to, who have autistic children or kids with ADHD in their class, often feel overwhelmed. Teaching can be challenging, but with the addition of children with special needs, and limited resources, they feel out of their depth.

Learning mindfulness won't change the classroom or the education system, but it will help you tap into your 'mindful teacher' within; the intuitive and creative mind that offers solutions to the situations you face. It may help you become more flexible with the needs of children who don't fit into the system. There are times when one-to-one support is best for that child and on other occasions, integrating that child into a class is best for all. Your mindfulness practice helps you see that these children are signposting you towards more creative and positive solutions; they are giving you the opportunity to change your way of thinking.

## Centering thought for your personal meditation practice

What do my children teach me?

## 2. CHANGING PERCEPTIONS OF SPECIAL NEEDS... MINDFULLY

*"Once you label me, you negate me."*

*Soren Kierkegaard, Philosopher*

Let's consider our perception of the words 'disability' or 'special needs'. Do you consider yourself to have a disability? If you are reading this book while wearing glasses or contact lenses, you do; without these inventions you would find it difficult to read. Your disability has been identified and glasses, contact lenses, eBook readers and voice readers are all gadgets that help you to live as if you had fully functioning eyes.

Children with autism are identified as having additional support needs. If they have sensory processing disorder (SPD), the world is a challenging place. They can have many over-stimulating experiences which leave them feeling very stressed. This makes it difficult for them to negotiate normal daily tasks that you and I take for granted. A trip to the supermarket, with its bright lights and colours, loud sounds, busy with staff and customers, contrasting music in aisles and shiny surfaces that reflect light must feel like torture for a child with SPD. Noise-cancelling earphones, originally designed to reduce the interference of background noise when we listen to music, are being used to help these children in environments with distressing levels of noise. This device enables helps them to negotiate their environment more peacefully.

New inventions are being created all the time for children on the spectrum. Chairs in class that have the ability to 'hug' the child as they sit (as the pressure helps them to feel secure and calm) or seats that have bicycle pedals attached under the desk to help children who require constant movement to feel calm and connected; allowing them to 'move' without disrupting others and yet focus on the lesson and the teacher.

## Limiting perceptions

Our perception of a 'disabled' child can also limit them. If we believe that a child with autism can't be independent, then we will act and behave as if this is the truth. But if we didn't believe this, our actions could be different and thus our influence on that child's abilities would be too. Sometimes our fearful thoughts can hold us back from recognising their abilities. The thoughts and feelings that generate that perception can either enable or disable them.

One of my friends was born with Still's Disease - a form of arthritis she had from childhood. As she grew older, her spine crumbled. She had to have a titanium loop in her neck to hold it up. Despite this debilitating disease, her parent's encouraged her to perceive herself as 'able' to do what others do; and she did. She had a family of four, a career, and she travelled. She would often talk about her parent's perception and how this empowered her.

Another friend, when her son with Down Syndrome was a young child, was told by specialists to give him trainers with Velcro fasteners, as they felt it would be too difficult and frustrating for him to tie his own shoe laces. She mindfully taught him, through daily practice, how to tie his shoelaces. It took him the better part of a year to master it, but well worth the time and effort! Now 36 years old, this young man has mastered many things in life and enjoys a great degree of independence in his community.

I have met many people who initially resisted the idea that children with ADHD or on the spectrum could learn to meditate. Intuitively I knew they could and I now have many examples confirming that they can, from my own professional practice or through our Connected Kids tutors worldwide.

If we are mindful when we perceive this world of children with disabilities, we will not limit them by our own fearful thoughts or emotions, but empower them with a solid foundation of resources and self belief. This will help them accept themselves as different, but not disabled.

I use different terms in this book; disabled children, children with disabilities, special needs or additional support needs, autistic children or children on the autistic spectrum. My intention is to show that how we communicate can influence our perception of children's abilities. I explore this in more depth in Chapter 3 – *'Practising mindfulness to teach meditation'*.

## The Autistic Spectrum

When we talk about the autistic spectrum, we say 'a child on the spectrum'. What we forget is that we are on that spectrum. The symptoms of autism indicate where a child sits on the spectrum but there are many people in the world who have behaviours that may have been diagnosed as high functioning autism had this label existed. Our position on the spectrum influences our perception of the world and how we interact with it. Every one of us has our own unique experience and children with autism are no different. They connect to the world through their neurodiversity (natural variation of the human genome) which affects their perception and experiences. We can support and honour this neurodiversity with meditation.

Our 'internal wiring' determines which signals we can pick up. Some of the information comes via our 5 physical senses that feeds the nervous system and influences our body. Some of it comes through our 'sensitivity' to energy - tuning in where others don't. Children with autism can tune in to information that we can't. This sensitivity makes life a challenge; some struggle to cope because of the heavy interference through the chemicals in food, electromagnetic fields of technology or the mixed *'energy signals' they perceive from those around them. This makes them feel anxious and stressed. When we teach children with autism how to meditate, they reduce that feeling of stress, feel more connected, relaxed and able to negotiate the intense world of information that they perceive.

*This is where we respond saying "yes, I'm fine" but really we don't *feel* ok...the energy of our emotions and thoughts are being suppressed because of social conditioning – causing conflict between what we say and what autistic children can sense.

## The impact of stress

Whether meditation is for you or your children, it helps to reduce the impact of chronic stress. Stress has a large part to play in the learning and development of our brains.

In the *Calm Kids* book, I discuss stress in more detail (and how it affects children) pointing out that stress is a normal function of the human body which is designed to keep us alive. It becomes a problem when we don't move out of our stress response (fight/flight/freeze) and become locked in a state of chronic stress; a state of high alert.

If children feel stressed they struggle to absorb new information. They can no longer think rationally or creatively - they simply react. The more we 'push', the more children may run away (flight), daydream or zone out (freeze) or become angry (fight).

## Stress affects learning abilities

The stress response can be triggered by a lack of physical balance which will affect chldren's learning. A book called 'Smart Moves: Why Learning Is Not All In Your Head" by Carla Hannaford PhD explains that balance is influenced by the vestibular system; through the ears we have an internal GPS to help navigate our body through space, locate limbs, balance the head and coordinate both sides of the body.

When a child is feeling physically balanced, their nervous system supports their ability to learn; if not, they are stuck in survival mode - the stress response.

A child with autism can feel very threatened (and therefore stressed) from early on in their life through his sensitivity to the world around him. The world may appear very 'fluid' and this causes him stress. He may adapt coping routines to help him identify patterns in the world. Hand flapping is now recognised as a 'stim' calming technique that children use to help them feel more balanced. When there is a change to their environment or routine, many parents tell me how challenging this is for their kids; it can stimulate the stress response with difficult consequences.

Children with ADHD are in a state of stress as they are ungrounded. This makes it difficult for them to absorb information and learn. Kids with ADHD are moving to try and *ground* the body for balance.

We often see this movement as disruptive to learning, but they need to do this in order to feel balanced and able to learn (hence the school desks with cycling pedals as I mentioned earlier). Some recent findings present the health benefits of 'earthing'.

> *"Emerging evidence shows that contact with the Earth—whether being outside barefoot or indoors connected to grounded conductive systems—may be a simple, natural, and yet profoundly effective environmental strategy against chronic stress, ANS dysfunction, inflammation, pain, poor sleep, disturbed HRV, hypercoagulable blood, and many common health disorders, including cardiovascular disease."*

*Source:* "Earthing: Health Implications of Reconnecting the Human Body to the Earth's Surface Electrons" JEPH Volume 2012 - see 'Resources'

Moving meditation, like yoga, helps children develop a stronger core and balance; this reduces stress and improves their ability to absorb new information. Once in this more balanced state, they are able to practise seated meditation which helps them how to focus and filter out some of the stress triggers. Children learn how to be connected, balanced and able to cope with change.

## Intuitive solutions

When we want to teach children meditation, there is no 'one size fits all'. We have to develop bespoke mindful activities that suit their needs. The beauty of meditation is that it can do just that.

> *"I have done (almost) daily meditation/breath work, some by myself and some with Annabel. We have sat together a few times cross-legged, holding hands and concentrating on our breath, blowing away thoughts that pop into our busy or worried minds. We have had great fun with this doing a lot of blowing and laughing at the start of the sessions."*

> Megan, Mum (case study)

As you learn how to adapt meditation for children with special needs, your own mindful journey unfolds and your empathy grows. This book is just the start (or the continuation) of your creative journey; inspiring you and your children to co-create mindfulness tools and practices together.

## Centering thought for your personal meditation practice

How do I accept my child's abilities?

## 3. PRACTISING MINDFULNESS TO TEACH MEDITATION

*"Mindfulness is simply being aware of what is happening right now without wishing it were different; enjoying the pleasant without holding on when it changes (which it will); being with the unpleasant without fear that it will always be this way (which it won't)."*

*James Baraz, Author of 'Awakening Joy'*

Through our Connected Kids programme, we spend time showing adults how to 'check in' with their intentions, their body, their mind and their feelings in case these influence the meditation they are teaching to children.

Often we don't realise the influence of our thoughts such as "I am the adult and I must be in control". When we are teaching meditation we are guiding, not controlling. Practising mindfulness as we teach, gives us a moment to let go and accept any negative emotions or thoughts arising within; it helps us to release any need to control the meditation, our children or the outcome.

### Mindful communication

What we say and what we *think* we are saying can be two different things.

I was walking my dog past our local nursery. A group of three-year-olds came running and picked up a handful of gravel with the intent to throw it.

The nursery assistant saw them (and us) and said, "Watch, there's a dog." The children threw the gravel (fortunately missing us) but I could see the look of disbelief on the assistant's face.

I realised that what she had *meant* to say was "don't throw stones". Even though she had used a warning tone, her words were factual and it was clear that she was unaware of this; an example of non-mindful communication.

Being mindful helps us to be present when communicating with children. With children on the spectrum, it is especially important to be clear and specific.

We unintentionally (without mindfulness) teach children irony or sarcasm, but autistic children don't understand this. They can be very literal in their use of language, and our sarcasm confuses them. It doesn't support clear, mindful communication.

## The power of perception

When we practise mindfulness, we become more aware of our own perception and how it influences our interpretation of the world around us; colouring the facts, or projecting our fears and thoughts onto our children. When we recognise this, we will listen and talk much more mindfully. With mindfulness, we can develop greater understanding and compassion when we see our children and teenagers struggling to process and interact with the world in the only way they know how. It can also teach us that peace is an inside job; we can't control the world, but we can take responsibility and control of our own emotions and thoughts.

If your child shouts at you and this makes you feel irritated or upset, the seed of this was already in you; they didn't cause the irritation, they fanned irritation 'flame' that was already present. The 'flame' was there due to your perception of other stresses (your partner, job or financial issues) and it came to light when your button was pressed.

If we teach children meditation, they aren't drawn into the drama of other people's lives but can connect with their inner guidance to determine the feeling, notice what triggered it and to let it pass with mindfulness; this is a powerful life skill.

*"Several years ago I had attended one of the first Connected Kids classes, convinced of the benefits of meditation through my own experience of it and keen to try some techniques with my own children. I was utterly terrified by the prospect of delivering a meditation to one of my children and have them 'reject' me in some way, either laughing at my complete incompetence or being completely bored and disinterested in something that was quite important to me.*

*My relationship with my two eldest children, who were still of primary school age at the time, was full of resistance. I attempted to coerce my children into the behaviour that I wanted, parenting them as I had been parented myself. Somehow I had become a carbon-copy of my own mother in spite of my own best efforts. My attempts at controlling my children (threats, naughty-step, rewarding good behaviour and punishing the 'bad' by removing privileges) were met sometimes with unwilling compliance, and often with outright rebellion! My journey of teaching meditation to my children has been a journey of self-discovery indeed.*

*I realised that we are being taught just as much as we are teaching, learning that our need for control usually comes from our fears, and learning to let go, one at a time, of the habitual patterns of parenting that I had so unconsciously been exhibiting. My children reflected back to me each of my beliefs about myself, and their resistance to me reflected my own inner-resistance and my lack of self-belief.*

*Teaching my children meditation became a joyful process of trial-and-error and empowering my children to make choices... like all children, there are some things that they enjoy and some things they don't find so captivating and enjoyable. It was starting to become so clear that the time we spent together deliberately cultivating a softer way of being together was transforming our relationship.*

*Together, we started to explore our feelings with curiosity and began to embrace a kinder and less judgemental attitude. I was starting to be able to let go of needing things to be a certain way, and became less worried about what people might think of how my children behaved. We were healing each other, one heartfelt meditation at a time."*

Heather Mackenzie, Connected Kids Trainer

Author of 'The Awakening Child'

This short meditation can be useful to help bring you and your kids into the moment.

## 'Being present' mindful meditation

*Sit or stand in a comfortable position (with good contact with the ground through your feet or the base of your spine).*

*Eyes can be open but have a soft gaze. Or you can close them.*

*Notice where you are in this moment. (Are you thinking about something that has happened? Or thinking about something that is to happen?)*

*Now take your mind back to the beginning of your day when you woke up.*

*Try to imagine this using all your senses (touch, smell, sound, sight and taste).*

*How did you feel when you woke up?*

*Now 'walk' yourself through your day - different activities, who you spoke to (and again bringing in the senses when you can).*

*At different moments in your day, just stop in your imagination and check in with how you were feeling at this point (do this for as many points in the day as you can remember).*

*Don't linger – imagine you are watching it on a movie screen with a bit of detachment.*

*Keep doing this until you bring your attention into this moment, this breath, these feelings and where your body stands/sits.*

*As you breathe out, let the 'past' of the day go (imagine it 'draining' down into the ground and as it does, you feel lighter inside with each breath).*

*Bring a physical smile to your face... and notice where you feel that in your body.*

*Open your eyes and continue to experience your day - mindfully.*

## Mindfulness as a life skill for children

Mindfulness is about asking children to pay attention to how they feel, what they are thinking and how their body feels in the moment. Paying attention to the breath and the five physical senses helps children to be aware of the 'here and now' and the world around them.

At first, children may be too young to learn. However the more we (the adults) practise it, the more it will help us to stay in the present and perceive the facts rather than becoming involved in any dramas. Plus children will witness and learn this behaviour from our mindful actions.

If stressed, repeating the following phrase with a single, deep breath helps you to be mindful when communicating/listening. The only 'real' thing is the breath and by focusing on it you can calm your mind and feelings. While repeating the words, try to visualise or feel the breath from beginning to end. It is useful to practise this frequently before, during and after the incident (and regularly throughout your day).

## Mindful Breath Meditation

*Shift your full attention to your chest.*

*On the in-breath (thinking)...*

*"Breathing in, I know I am breathing in";*

*On the out-breath (thinking)...*

*"Breathing out, I know I am breathing out.*

*(Repeat for several breaths while paying really close attention to the breath).*

*Now change it to...*

*"Breathing in, I know this moment shall pass";*

*"Breathing out, I know this moment shall pass".*

(Repeat for several breaths and pay particular attention to the 'out breath' as this engages our parasympathetic system, helping the nervous system to relax.)

## Mindful listening

One of my colleagues told me about a child with special needs who had a 15 second delay in processing and answering a question. The parents didn't realise this and were struggling to communicate with their child (as was the therapist who was helping them). When it was eventually discovered they realised how frustrating it was for their child to be asked question after question without the time to answer because no-one waited long enough to hear; mindful listening would have helped.

Another example comes from one of our 'Connected Kids' tutors who taught meditation to an eight-year-old boy. The boy was asked to choose a colour for his meditation. He chose 'blue', which links to our expression of choices and emotions. *(See* Chapter 5 - 'Teaching meditation with energy awareness'*)*

Afterwards, the boy spoke to his family about something that had happened on a school visit to the sports centre. In the changing rooms, everyone was getting dressed so that they could catch the bus. The boy was taking his time and the teacher came in to tell them to hurry. Although what she meant to say was "hurry up, so we can catch the bus!" What she actually said was "right - we're going!"

On hearing the words "we're going", the boy started to feel anxious because he thought he was going to be left behind, although there was no real danger of this.

Even though the meditation theme wasn't specifically about releasing this anxiety, it helped him to process it so he could express his feelings, and give his parents the opportunity to reassure him. But you can imagine how this feeling could have continued to affect his perception of the teacher if he hadn't had a chance to reflect and express it. Mindful communication was missing (the teacher) but mindful listening and the meditation helped.

For teenagers, mindfulness is important as it helps them to acknowledge feelings and emotions and process them in a safe way. It teaches them to be present and accepting of themselves and others, especially as their bodies go through immense change and pressure.

Mindfulness also helps children who use computer games, or if their imaginations are influenced by negative or stressful images. Through our work, we have found that if a child has experienced negative imagery through computers or media, that this affects their sleep patterns and sends them into the stress response. It also influences the meditation experience. Although initially they can experience a peaceful moment in the meditation, the mind is so accustomed to negative images that these pop in and disrupt the calmness. By teaching these children mindfulness (helping them to anchor their awareness into their body and breath), we can show them how to have a stronger focus while letting go of negative thoughts.

*"I had a teen that slept through the night for the first time in 18 months after just a few days of doing a 'body scan' meditation."*

Linsey Denham

One of the essential tools we teach in class is called the 'Namaste Bow' - this helps us to practise mindful listening and communication - see Chapter 14 - 'Developing emotional awareness'.

## Mindful problem solving

When we teach children meditation, we are not trying to force them to become 'perfect' or 'quiet' children. We're trying to help them find a way to process, express and accept what they are feeling and thinking in a safe and calm way. When this happens, their stress levels reduce.

Meditation can also help to release a worry or fear, or to find a creative solution to that problem. Try taking a problem into meditation with the intention of looking at it from a different perspective.

If you and your children learn to meditate on something that is a problem, and sit down to mindfully talk about it afterwards, you will be amazed by the creative solutions and insights that arise through the creative power of your minds and from sharing these different perspectives. Even if there is nothing to share, the meditation can still help process thoughts and feelings and bring peace into a difficult situation. In Chapter 6 - 'Connecting to Heart Centre Intelligence' there is a 'problem solving' meditation you may like to try.

## Mindfulness for teaching meditation

Our own mindfulness is essential in the process of teaching children and teens meditation. If you practise mindfulness as you teach, it helps you to listen to the 'mindful teacher' within, tune in to your child's energy and helps you intuitively choose and tailor a mindful activity and words that is most balancing for your child's needs.

Working on the case studies for this book, our first step was to meditate on the issues. We worked mindfully to tune in to the children's (and parents') energy, we listened to our 'mindful teacher' within, and developed mindful activities and meditation ideas that intuitively felt best for those children. We encouraged parents to practise mindfulness which helped reduce stress and gave them the confidence to adapt or change our suggestions.

## Mindfulness for the family

If your child is autistic, has ADHD or other additional support needs and you are not yet at the stage where it is possible to teach him meditation, then it's still important to meditate with siblings, your partner and anyone else who comes into contact with your child, to see if there are ways in which you can support each other during challenging times.

Mindful practise with your family helps everyone to acknowledge their thoughts, how to observe them and let them pass so that they can come back to a point of balance in each breath and within the body. If there are strong emotions simmering beneath the surface, meditation can help them to feel and embrace them in the heart. The facts of outside circumstances won't change, but the way you and your family feel about them can change through a mindful perspective. Having the opportunity to be heard will help your family become more compassionate towards their brother, sister or child. There may be no direct solution, but this mindful activity can be very healing.

## Centering thought for your personal meditation practice

How can I pay more attention to the 'mindful teacher' within?

## 4. THE BENEFITS OF MEDITATION - MEDICAL RESEARCH

*"Recent research on meditation and mindfulness has contributed significantly to a new understanding of the brain's capacity for change in response to experience."*

*Zoran Josipovic, PhD, Adjunct Assistant Professor, New York University*

Although opinions are rapidly changing, it helps society accept the idea of teaching meditation to children if there are some tangible, measurable benefits. This part of the book is dedicated to realising this as fact; that meditation helps on a physical, emotional and mental level.

The brain is a good place to begin. It is amazing in that it connects us neurologically to the rest of our body. In the last 15 years, research has helped us understand how the brain works and how its complex relationship can influence our emotions, our hormones, our physical well-being and our capacity to learn.

At the time of writing, there is a growing consensus that conditions such as autism and ADHD have a neurological basis. Seeing how the brain works and how a child's mind develops will help us consider how practising meditation could have positive effects for those with or without special needs. It will also help us to adapt meditation to the abilities of the children we teach.

The following excerpts are from an excellent article by neurologist, Dr Judy Willis, on the functions of the brain. Following each point, I include my own observations about the connection between brain development and practising meditation.

### 'What you should know about your brain'

by Dr Judy Willis

*"Although the brain is an amazing organ, it's not equipped to process the billions of bits of information that bombard it every second. Filters in your brain protect it from becoming overloaded. These filters control the information flow so that only approximately 2,000 bits of information per second enter the brain."*

This may explain why autistic children find it difficult to cope with the outside world. Sensory processing disorders mean they are unable to filter the information coming into their brain. I believe that being overwhelmed with information activates the stress response. Meditation helps us teach children how to relax, focus and filter information with mindfulness, helping to counteract the effects of the stress response.

## The thinking brain and the reactive brain

*"Once sensory information enters the brain, it's routed to one of two areas: (1) The pre-frontal cortex, what we might call the thinking brain, which can consciously process and reflect on information; or (2) the lower, automatic brain, what we might call the reactive brain, which reacts to information instinctively rather than through thinking. The pre-frontal cortex is actually only 17% of your brain; the rest makes up the reactive brain."*

The pre-frontal cortex is what we engage when we learn how to meditate. It helps us respond to life mindfully, rather than reacting to it. If children learn to engage this, they make more mindful decisions rather than reactive responses when faced with life challenges; learning to self-regulate and develop emotional intelligence.

*"When you are not stressed by negative emotions, you can control what information makes it into your brain. By calming your brain, you can control which sensory data from your environment your brain lets in or keeps out and influence which information gets admitted to your pre-frontal cortex."*

Meditation helps to calm our mind, our emotions and our body. This can help children respond to life in a calmer, more centred way, rather than living in a state of stress and simply reacting. It can also aid learning and development if the brain and body are calmer.

> *"When your stress levels are down and your interest is high, the most valuable information tends to pass into your thinking brain."*

Meditation teaches us how to keep our stress levels in a more balanced state, and enhances our ability to learn. This is helpful for children's brain development which occurs until their early 20's.

> *"When you are anxious, sad, frustrated or bored, brain filters conduct sensory information from the world around you into your reactive brain. These reactive brain systems do one of three things with the information: ignore it; fight against it as a negative experience (sending signals that may cause you to act inappropriately); or avoid it (causing you to daydream). If information gets routed to this reactive brain, it's unlikely your brain will truly process the information or remember it."*

Meditation helps us to bring information into the pre-frontal cortex and help 'disengage' the reactive brain, thus helping us to engage with the world in a more centered way. It will also allow our children to improve their learning development and process and release negative emotions, helping them to develop emotional intelligence.

*Source:* 'What you should know about your brain' by Dr Judy Willis. See 'Resources' for link to the full article.

(Please note that the information above, other than the sources quoted, is based on my own experience and opinions; it is therefore theoretical and cannot be used as a medical diagnosis or treatment).

## Research into meditation

Scientific studies are providing the evidence of how meditation affects our bodies and our sense of well-being, as the following articles illustrate.

## Reducing anxiety

In June 2013, the Wake Forest Baptist Medical Centre published a report in the journal *'Social Cognitive and Affective Neuroscience'*. The report concluded that;

> *"Research and technology have advanced to the point where scientists can observe the way in which meditation affects the brain to reduce anxiety."*

Researchers followed 15 healthy volunteers with normal levels of everyday anxiety. The participants did not have previous meditation experience or diagnosed anxiety disorders.

All subjects participated in four 20-minute classes to learn a technique known as mindfulness meditation. The majority of participants reported a decrease in anxiety, some by as much as 39%.

The researchers discovered that meditation-related anxiety relief is associated with activation of the areas of the brain involved with executive-level function (the anterior cingulate cortex and ventromedial pre-frontal cortex).

During meditation, there was more activity in the ventromedial pre-frontal cortex, the area of the brain that controls worrying. In addition, when activity increased in the anterior cingulate cortex - the area that governs thinking and emotion - anxiety decreased.

Fadel Zeidan, author of the study, said: "Mindfulness is premised on sustaining attention in the present moment and controlling the way we react to daily thoughts and feelings."

Source:'Meditation That Eases Anxiety? Brain Scans Show Us How' www.psychcentral.com, June 2013

One of our case studies involved Annabel (age 7) who was suffering from anxiety attacks. She had separation anxiety from her mum, and often felt nauseous when she was at school. School assembly with lots of children in one room was overwhelming for her. Annabel had to deal with a girl who bullied her at school, which knocked her self confidence. (You can read the full case study in Part 3 of this book).

> "Annabel was upset the other night about feeling excluded from school, and after we had a good, calm chat about life and friendships, we did some breathing together, breathing in bright, warm happiness and breathing out negative, black things in our life. She was asleep within a couple of minutes. I think it's a combination of being used to the whole concept of breath calming us down and practising it in her yoga class and at home."

> Megan, Mum (case study)

## Reducing Stress

In the USA, a study of 66 people (18 to 30 years) found that 25 minutes of daily mindfulness meditation could alleviate psychological stress.

Source: "Only 25 Minutes of Mindfulness Meditation Alleviates Stress, According to Carnegie Mellon Researchers"; Carnegie Mellon University, Pittsburgh, July 2014

Regular meditation was shown to help reduce the stress hormone, cortisol, in high school students who practised meditation daily with yoga classes.

Source: "TM Chills out a High School"; Newhaven Independent, April 2014,

## Improving attention skills and reducing lapses in attention

Neuroscientists have documented the way in which meditation impacts on brain activity itself. For example, meditation has been associated with decreased activity in undesirable brain functions responsible for lapses of attention and disorders such as anxiety and ADHD.

Meditation has also been linked to dramatic changes in electrical brain activity, namely increased theta and alpha activity using an EEG; an electroencephalogram which detects the electrical activity of the brain. Theta and alpha brain waves are associated with wakeful and relaxed attention. The latter is what we cultivate when we teach children meditation. The more relaxed the brain (stress-free), the more easily it can absorb information.

*Sources:* US National Library of Medicine, 'Meditation experience is associated with increased cortical thickness'; Lazar, Kerr et al, 2005; National Academy of Sciences in the United States of America, 'Meditation experience is associated with differences in default mode network activity and connectivity', Brewer, Worhunsky et al, 2011; Life & Style (New Zealand) 2013.


## Improving the ability to process information (study and learn)

Research at the University of California in Los Angeles has illustrated that meditation can help strengthen the brain.

Eileen Luders, an assistant professor at the UCLA Laboratory of Neuro Imaging, and colleagues, have found that long-term meditation practitioners have larger amounts of gyrification which is "folding" of the cortex. This may allow the brain to process information faster than people who do not meditate.

*Source:* 'Meditation strengthens the brain'; Newsroom, University of California, Los Angeles, March 2012

## Helping brain function in autism

The brain has a few useful 'chemical messengers' that help it to transmit information.

**Dopamine** helps the brain to perform its functions. It affects sleep, mood, motivation and learning. When dopamine is absent, it is suggested it can lead to issues such as ADHD.

**Oxytocin** is formed in the hypothalamus in the brain and helps with the birthing process and breast feeding. However, it also influences feelings of trust, recognition and affection. It helps regulate sleep, mood and appetite. A deficiency of oxytocin has pointed towards depression and anxiety. It has been found to enhance brain function in children with autism.

**Endorphins** are seen as a natural painkiller and can give a feeling of well-being (e.g. we release endorphins into our bloodstream when we laugh or exercise).

A growing body of research confirms that meditation and mindfulness can help positively influence the above neurotransmitters and their associated brain functions.

*Sources:* Meditation's positive residual effects', 'Turn down the volume' , 'Eight weeks to a better brain'; Harvard University Gazette, January 2011 - April 2012. 'Oxytocin enhances brain function in children with autism'; Hindawi Publishing Corporation, April 201. 'Increased dopamine tone during meditation-induced change of consciousness'; John F Kennedy Institute, Denmark, Imperial College School of Medicine, London, Danish Epilepsy Hospital, Denmark, April 2002.

## The power of the mind

Dr David Hamilton, author of 'It's the Thought that Counts' gives some examples of why the mind has such control over the body. Dr Hamilton worked in the pharmaceutical industry in 1995. He witnessed the 'placebo effect' in drug trials, and this led him to research the power of the mind.

*"In 1950, a scientific report was published in the Journal of Clinical Investigation that described a powerful placebo effect in a group of 33 pregnant women who were having morning sickness.*

*The women took part in a trial where they were told that they would be given a drug that would stop their nausea and vomiting. This is what is called 'suggestion'. It was 'suggested' that the drug would work. To make the results even more precise, the scientists asked the women to swallow a small instrument that would allow them to measure stomach contractions that came with the waves of nausea.*

*After they took the drug, the women reported that their nausea and vomiting had stopped and the researchers also noted that the contractions, measured by the swallowed instruments, had also stopped. So the drug had been very successful.*

*But actually, the women were not given a drug as they had been told. Instead, they had been given a drug that should have made them even more sick - syrup of ipecac."*

The author goes on to talk about how we can influence our genetics by what we think:

*"In reality, our intentional and unintentional visualisations inspire DNA twenty-four hours a day, three hundred and sixty five days a year. We are simply unaware of the process. So we continually affect our genetic code and the nature of the effect is simply down to the nature of our thoughts, feelings, attitudes, beliefs and intentions."*

*Source:*'It's the Thought that Counts: Why Mind Over Matter Really Works' by Dr David Hamilton, pub. Hay House, 2008

## Putting this knowledge into practice

In the Connected Kids programme, we practise a mindfulness exercise that brings a notable physiological response in the body using the power of the imagination. It prompts the question "can we affect our stress levels, both positively and negatively, by how we think?"

Children today have higher stress levels. Perhaps it is due to over exposure of technology, increased chemicals in the diet and the current pace of life. This is the society we have created for our children and although meditation isn't a cure, it offers some relief from these stressors. It has the potential to positively impact on children's learning, brain development and emotional intelligence.

(See 'Resources'- for a link to full articles/research sources. As links on the internet can become obsolete, please visit www.teachchildrenmeditation.com where we will endeavour to keep them updated).

## Centering thought for your personal meditation practice

What benefits can meditation bring to children with special needs?

# 5. TEACHING MEDITATION WITH ENERGY AWARENESS

*"A human being is a part of the whole called by us universe, a part limited in time and space. He experiences himself, his thoughts and feeling as something separated from the rest, a kind of optical delusion of his consciousness. This delusion is a kind of prison for us, restricting us to our personal desires and to affection for a few persons nearest to us. Our task must be to free ourselves from this prison by widening our circle of compassion to embrace all living creatures and the whole of nature in its beauty."*

*Albert Einstein, Physicist*

We study the world through science but there is another way to consider the positive impact of meditation through our awareness of energy.

The idea of 'energy' seems mystical and holistic. Yet we can refer to quantum physics to help us understand energy. Physical matter isn't solid, but made up of tiny atoms (vortices of energy, spinning and vibrating). So the chair you are sitting on seems solid, but it is a vibrating mass of atoms giving the impression of being solid. Our bodies, the world around us and the universe are all vibrating in this way; all made from the same materials, all connected through energy.

Meditation gives us access to experiencing this energy that goes beyond our physical senses and interpretation. There are many books written about this, but how we experience energy is a unique journey. From my personal, meditation journey, I know that we *all* have the ability to sense energy; as children we knew this. As adults, we simply need to remember.

Thoughts and feelings have energy which affect not only our own energy but send out energy in waves affecting the world around us. These are experienced by others, particularly children. If I'm in a bad mood, I might say or do nothing physically that gives this impression, but you may sense it on some level through your energy 'antennae'. The well-known saying, "I could cut the atmosphere with a knife" sums up the feeling someone experiences when they sense this feeling; the energy of those thoughts and feelings from their environment.

The difficulty for children (and many adults) is that when they pick up on the emotions and thoughts of other people, they aren't sure what is happening or how to process it. The sensing but 'not knowing/understanding' can alert their stress response. All children can feel the energy of their parents without a word being spoken. We often try to protect our children from 'bad news', but they can feel the energy of an adult's emotions and thoughts that surround them. If a parent or adults tells a child everything is okay, but the child can feel that it isn't okay, this causes confusion and fear. For children with autism I believe their ability to sense this disparity is more acute.

## The energy system of the chakras

Originating in healing texts that date back thousands of years, the chakra energy system gives us a structure to help interpret energy. I refer to this system in my courses as it is a useful tool for teaching meditation.

'Chakra' is a Sanskrit word meaning 'spinning wheel of energy'. Sanskrit is one of the root languages of our human species that originated several thousand years ago. These energy centres are believed to be gateways or portals through which we allow energy to enter and exit the body. Each vibrates with an associated colour, and each governs certain aspects of our physical, mental, emotional and spiritual well-being.

*(If you are interested in the general development of children's chakras, my book, 'Calm Kids', explains this in more detail. In this chapter, I*

*include specific information that is useful for teaching mediation, managing your own energy and the chakras of children on the autistic spectrum).*

In our energy system there are seven main chakras. Each chakra holds a unique collection of energy that pertains to our thoughts, feelings, physical actions and spiritual influence. Like files on a computer stick, we gather this information from the moment we are conceived through every life experience. We use these files to run our 'programmes' which help us to interact and make sense of the world in which we live.

Many of the original 'programmes' we run are set through our childhood experiences and we re-run the programme with each similar life event. Mindfulness helps us explore which 'files' need updated or deleted.

If we study our personal energy through meditation, it gives us a way to develop compassion and understanding for our own journey, the world we live in and who we share it with.

The following chart gives you some background to the energy centres and the influence they have when teaching meditation. The chart is a starting point and not the complete picture. It will be your own chakra meditation practice which will help you to 'understand' what chakras are and how awareness of them can help you to deliver a heartfelt, authentic and healing meditation for your children. There is no hierarchical structure to the system - each chakra plays an important part in our personal development.

## Chakra chart - summary

I have included the colours here as colour can be a meditation tool as explained in Chapter 8 - 'Working with colour'.

The Chakra Energy System

crown

brow

throat

heart

solar plexus

sacral

root

© Connected Kids Ltd

| Chakra – position, colour and aspects | Influence when teaching meditation |
|---|---|
| **Crown** - top of the head - white/magenta - big picture/meaning of life/religious beliefs | Offers big picture inspiration to help guide the meditation or a mindful activity. |
| **Brow** - slightly above and between the eyebrows - dark blue/purple - imagination/intuition/thoughts | Translates our 'intuitive inspiration' into ideas or concepts that we can use to create a meditation. |
| **Throat** - base of the throat - sky blue - expression of feelings/honesty with self and | Helps us to express our heartfelt and inspired ideas through |

| others | words. |
|---|---|
| **Heart** – centre of chest above sternum - green (can also be pink) - expression of love/gratitude | Our ability to 'tune in' and sense the energy of a child/teen takes place through the heart centre. Teaching from here, we learn to trust our instincts. The energy of heart-felt compassion can have a healing and balancing effect through the meditation. |
| **Solar Plexus** - centre and beneath chest - yellow - control/self esteem/judgement/power. | As the adult, we are accustomed to being in control yet in teaching meditation we learn to 'let go' and trust (heart centre) the words and inspiration that guide the meditation. The solar plexus can struggle with the fear of 'not being in control'. |
| **Sacral** - just beneath the navel - orange - physical expression of creativity/playfulness/spontaneity. | Teaching meditation to kids isn't a condensed version of adult meditation. We can make it more playful and fun to engage their interest. The sacral has a large influence on the energy of relationships. It links strongly with the throat centre. With teens, we can transform our relationships with them through authentic and mindful talking and listening. |

| | |
|---|---|
| **Root** - beneath the base of the spine - red - grounding/centred/feeling safe and protected. | If we are grounded when teaching, we feel safe enough to let go, to trust our heart centre wisdom and allow whatever outcome occurs. |

## Exploring the chakras for teaching meditation

### Crown chakra

The crown chakra is our connection with the energy of the universe; I call it our 'divine connection'. This is where we either accept (or don't) that there is more to life than meets the eye. It doesn't require us to believe that there is this connection (atheists and agnostics also have crown chakras!) The condition of the crown connection can influence how much we trust in a 'bigger picture' or of opening up to our spirituality. Our own meditation practice helps us to engage with the crown chakra. In teaching meditation, the initial focus isn't to make children spiritually aware. However a balanced crown centre can help them feel more in-tune with the universe. When a child reaches a stage in their mental development where they can embrace concepts such as religion and spirituality, they may explore this more consciously through meditation.

### Tips for balancing the crown chakra

Meditation and energy healing (such as Reiki) will help balance the crown chakra.

Guided meditation theme; Imagine yourself breathing in and out of the crown chakra, while visualising a beautiful flower opening to the light in the sky/universe – drawing this down into the body with each breath.

Remember that the practice of teaching meditation is healing for you too; as you teach meditation you are becoming more consciously aware of this divine connection. The fact that you have bought or are reading this book suggests that your crown chakra is active!

## Brow chakra

When we connect with the brow chakra, it allows us the opportunity to tap into our intuition and offers us useful insights and perspectives. Our personal meditation practice is helpful in balancing this energy centre.

The brow chakra is important in teaching meditation, because it gives us the opportunity to balance the logical expression of thoughts with our capacity to have creative thoughts. Our brow chakra gives us the intuitive idea; we might think of images and words to guide our meditation for a particular child, or we may feel inspired to try a different mindful practice. Initially when we become more aware of this intuition, we may reject it as 'just being our imagination'. The imagination is where creative solutions are found; not through logical analysis. For adults we can initially struggle letting go of the analysis and enjoying and trusting the intuitive imagination so we have to practise, practise and practise!

If we follow the meditation script created by another person, we are teaching meditation logically and give ourselves no room to bring in our intuitive creativity as we develop ideas or deliver meditations. If we are willing to trust our intuitive imagination in the brow chakra, then the words will flow more easily and the meditation will feel more suited to the (energetic) needs of the child.

## Tips for balancing the brow chakra

To increase your trust in your intuitive abilities, practise meditation! Take a moment to consider that every physical item in the room around you started as an idea or a (creative) thought in someone's mind. That person then made the decision to physically create it. They could easily have ignored that thought and what you see wouldn't exist.

If you find it difficult to embrace the creative imagination that is required for teaching meditation, read your child's books!

If you have a copy of my first book, 'Calm Kids', look at the section on writing meditation scripts. This is very similar to creative story writing, which will help you to trust your intuitive ability to create wonderful, personalised meditations for your children.

## Throat chakra

The throat centre helps us to express our emotional energy; to speak, draw, sing or write what we feel. Sometimes we have a fear of being hurt, rejected or of not being heard, and this emotion can be held in our throat chakra. If we are scared of expressing our true essence and our creativity, then we will hold ourselves back from teaching meditation to children. We often use food to control what we feel; forcing the emotions deep down inside or refusing to eat.

The throat chakra is naturally important in teaching meditation because children will be listening to the words we speak. However it is the heart centre energy behind the words that makes the difference. I occasionally find that children don't hear every word I say when I teach meditation; they may even go on a different journey, choosing images or a place that they prefer. This is absolutely fine! There is no right and wrong when teaching meditation: the person, young or old, will hear what they are meant to hear for their own healing and balance. Even though they may not appear to be listening, on a deeper level the vibration of sound from your voice, and your heartfelt intention, will connect to their energy.

(Children with a hearing impairment will still feel the energy of the words even if they can't hear them).

## Tips for balancing the throat chakra

To release blocked energy in your throat centre, you could try working with mandalas (see Chapter 10 - 'Mandala meditations for healing and balance'), singing or chanting a word, vowel or mantra such as 'Om'. You could write down what is bothering you and imagine saying this to the person who has upset you. You can also try 'the angry socks' release activity in Part 3 - Annabel Case study. Practising this will help energy to flow more easily in the throat centre. There is an important partnership between the sacral chakra and the throat which means that by expressing emotions, we will help the sacral come into balance.

## Heart chakra

When I'm teaching meditation, for me, this is the most important of all the chakras. When we work with the heart centre, we have no expectations or attachments to the outcome - just a positive intention combined with the wisdom of the open heart.

The heart centre has its own innate intelligence. It is the gateway for the universal energy to flow through us. This is the same energy and intelligence that 'instructs' the DNA in our bodies and influences our physical growth, just as it influences the shape, form, colour and texture of every other living organism. It also affects our mental development and emotional intelligence.

When teaching meditation, it is important to keep our awareness on the area of the heart centre (the centre of the chest). Take your attention to it as you speak, so that you 'feel' as well as 'see' the meditation in your imagination. Sometimes I guide students to place their hand on their heart centre as they speak. (I will tell you more about the role of the heart chakra for teaching meditation in Chapter 6 - 'Connecting to heart centre intelligence'.)

### Tips for balancing the heart chakra

Giving and receiving compliments, donating to charity, acts of kindness, sharing time/food/help with others or telling someone that we love them - with no expectations of what they will say in reply. Tell your children this often, and feel the words in your heart chakra; smile as you speak or meditate, and notice the sensation in your chest.

Keep a gratitude diary and write things down daily that you feel grateful for.

All of these steps will help you (and your children) have a more open heart chakra.

## Solar plexus chakra

This is a centre of mental and psychic energy. The solar plexus is where we hold the energy of our fears - our anxiety and our stress. The physical adrenal glands are located in this area, and these affect our 'fight, freeze or flight' response. We can pick up a lot of information through the solar plexus chakra; perhaps you will have heard the term 'gut instinct'. We can become very attached to the outcome, wanting life to be perfect. This makes it difficult to let go.

In teaching meditation, it is important for us to bring in an awareness of both the heart and the solar plexus chakras. This enables us to work with unconditional love while letting go of our fears of making a mistake. Letting go of these fears with awareness of each breath will help shift your energy from the attachment of the solar plexus to the non-attachment of the heart centre.

I have worked with a number of experienced meditation teachers and those that have the most impact let go of the need to be 'right' or in control; they work from the heart chakra. It can help if you place a hand on your chest and one on your solar plexus as a gentle reminder of these areas. I often find that when adults start to teach children meditation, they feel they should be 'in charge' of the meditation and the outcome. If we try to control this we are not teaching mindfully. The energy of control can be felt by the children and teenagers who sense it through your voice and your energy. As they feel this they will resist!

If you are struggling to let go of being in 'parent/teacher-mode' when teaching meditation, share the guiding experience with your children. Agree to lead the meditation at the start and finish (with attention on the breath and relaxing the body) but allow them to take you on the guided journey using their imagination. This role reversal can highlight the need for adults to let go and it also illustrates how creative children can be.

*"My 7-year old son has just delivered his first 30-minute meditation session to me and his brother. I'm so proud."*

Anna Kovacks, Connected Kids Tutor

## Tips for balancing the solar plexus chakra

The solar plexus is our core and our power centre. To balance this, and to give ourselves inner strength and courage, we can practise yoga and learn to breathe into our belly, expanding the torso with each in-breath and relaxing it on each out-breath. This breathing technique also engages the diaphragm in the body which (through the nervous system) helps send a relaxation signal to our brain; it's how we breathe when we are asleep.

Try practising spontaneity to help release the need to control.

If you're upset with a situation, especially one that involves your kids, don't pretend you are okay - speak honestly. We can share our feelings with children to show them that we are vulnerable and are still learning, too. This helps children to learn how to speak honestly and authentically.

If you are someone who has to do everything and you struggle to let people help you, practise now asking for help and accepting that your way is not the only way; this will help you to change the energy in your solar plexus chakra.

## Sacral chakra

The sacral chakra is the seat of our emotions, and in physical terms it is our creative centre: think about where your child came from. This is a joyful and playful energy centre, helping us to bring child-like fun and joy into our meditations. I can tell in class who has an active sacral chakra - they're the ones who laugh a lot and seem to enjoy life, instead of taking it all too seriously.

Allow your children to show you how to be playful and silly! Meditations for younger children should be engaging and fun, using the imagination in a light and joyful way to help the child feel at ease, happy and safe.

When teaching meditation, the sacral chakra works with the throat chakra, helping us to express our creativity and joy. Meditation can involve movement (such as yoga) or bring some laughter into the meditation, encouraging children to think of something silly or funny to focus on with their imagination. If you are taking the experience too seriously, think of something that makes you happy and smile as you speak so that you can feel this in your body.

### Tips for balancing the sacral chakra

To help you open out this energy centre in your body, try dancing to your favourite music. Take up Zumba or belly dancing! Yoga postures can help.

Try drawing or creative writing. Spend time with friends - laughing!

## Root chakra

The root chakra helps you feel safe and centred, and when you're teaching meditation this is important for both you and your child. If you aren't grounded you will feel overwhelmed. Being ungrounded makes it difficult to trust your intuition, to let go of the fear in the solar plexus and be in the moment as you speak from the heart.

When you are teaching meditation, ensure you have a solid contact with the ground beneath you, either through the base of your spine or the soles of your feet (remove shoes if you can). Try not to rush into teaching meditation but give yourself some time to prepare (yourself, the room and your children) so that you feel more centred before you begin.

### Tips for balancing the root chakra

Physical activities like walking and running - even cleaning the house - are very grounding for our energy.

If you feel ungrounded, you won't be able to think straight, so take yourself out for a walk, ideally in a natural environment where there are lots of trees as they have a grounding effect on your energy.

Ensure you have had enough sleep, food and water as this is physically nourishing and the root chakra ties in strongly with our physical wellbeing.

*Please note that any of these tips can help children balance the chakras.*

## The Aura

The energy field of the aura is a proven electromagnetic field that expands from our physical body, connecting it to our environment and each other. This energy field is influenced by the energy of thoughts and feelings, in addition to the physical body. It can expand towards those we love and retract from those that make us feel uncomfortable; consider how it feels when people 'enter your space' in an elevator or in conversation - especially if they stand 'too close'.

In meditation, our energy field can extend several feet away from the body, and those that practise for years can extend it for several miles. I believe that children have energy fields that are open, light and sensitive to the world around them. For some on the autistic spectrum, it is a struggle to cope with the energy of others if they can sense strong emotions. Due to their sensitivities, some children have learned to cope by 'disengaging' from those around them.

In one of our case studies, James (age 4) was undiagnosed but demonstrated some autistic issues and struggled with change. In energy terms, his energy field struggled to process and adapt to new environments; the 'new' energy he encountered activated his stress response due to the energy of new people and the environment. We developed a meditation to address this called 'the golden spacesuit'.

## The Golden Space Suit Meditation

*Spend a little bit of time helping your child to focus on the breath and relax.*

*Guide him to imagine he's wearing a golden space suit (you can physically help his imagination by guiding him to move as if were pulling it on - similar to a mime artist).*

*The suit has two special qualities which you guide your child to notice: it keeps him safe and shuts out excess noise or energy around him; and it feels like there are really heavy weights in the shoes, so like an astronaut he has to walk more slowly and he feels the weight making a stronger connection to the ground and the earth with every step.*

*With every step he feels stronger and safer (this can be done in an imaginative way or with him walking around the room).*

*"I think the golden space suit is a great idea. He really needs it at the moment as he has just started school which is a bit overwhelming for him. It has been perfect timing. He is very anxious so it helps him feel protected."*

Vanessa, Mum (case study)

## Centering thought for your personal meditation practice

Which chakra seems most in/out of balance in you? In your children?

# 6. CONNECTING TO HEART CENTRE INTELLIGENCE

*"Learning to teach from the heart was learning to trust myself and my intuition without fear of judgement from others and letting go of self-judgement. It was like going through growing pains. It was so worth it. The outcome of teaching from the heart is tremendous; I see real life changing results and the words just flow from me effortlessly now. The more you do it, the more you trust in yourself and your heart's wisdom"*

*Angela Connolly, Connected Kids Tutor*

The heart chakra plays an integral role in bringing healing and balance to our physical body and subtle energy. When we meditate with mindful awareness of the heart centre, it becomes a source of compassion, forgiveness, love and peace while bringing much insight and wisdom into what causes our own suffering, and the suffering of others. For teaching meditation with authenticity and integrity, it is essential that the words flow from our heart.

As children, I believe that we begin life with a heart centre which is fully open to the world; we embrace life with an innocence and curiosity. As we experience life, we face challenges and keeping the heart centre open becomes a test of our inner strength. If we allow our minds to dictate the course of life and we step away from the emotions, we seem to close the heart centre. This 'closing' can at first protect us from the pain, but it also limits our sense of joy and happiness; in other words we disconnect from the beauty of life we felt as a child.

When someone practices meditation and takes it deeper than the mind, we can touch the essence of the heart centre. Often this brings much emotion to the surface. Rather than being a negative experience, the tears represent a clearing of the blockage that has held that person back from feeling connected to life.

We choose to close the heart as it (initially) feels safer and easier to cope with feelings of grief or pain. However in the long term, it can bring us to a place that leaves us feeling empty and depressed. If children are taught how to process those difficult life challenges and emotions with more gentle, mindful awareness, then they will be able to accept that those emotions are a part of life. 'The Prophet', a beautiful book by Kahlil Gibran, helped me through my feelings of grief at the death of my mother.

*"Your joy is your sorrow unmasked. And the selfsame well from which your laughter rises was oftentimes filled with your tears. And how else can it be? The deeper that sorrow carves into your being, the more joy you can contain. When you are joyous, look deep into your heart and you shall find it is only that which has given you sorrow that is giving you joy. When you are sorrowful look again in your heart and you shall see that in truth you are weeping for that which has been your delight".*

## Processing emotions

As children, we learn from those around us how safe it is to emotionally process the experiences of life including pain, grief or sadness. If it isn't safe for the adults, then we learn to block the feeling. We end up as adults with what I call 'frozen heart centres', the emotions solidified by fear and pain. This pattern may continue for generations if children aren't given guidance and taught emotional intelligence; processing the energy of emotions in a safe and balanced way. With meditation, I have witnessed many children and adults learn to process, release and accept the difficult emotions they have tucked away inside; they have set themselves free.

The Institute of HeartMath has dedicated years of research into the influence of the heart, not just as a physical organ in the body, but as an intrinsic energy source within each human being. Researchers have examined the heart's connection to the brain and its ability to respond to different inner emotional states and stress influenced by, and influencing, our perception of the world.

One study looked at the connection between mothers and their babies through the electromagnetic field generated by the heart. Their preliminary results of a study conducted in August 2007 suggested that the heart was a source of information exchange between people and that it was influenced by the emotions. It went on to suggest that when a mother tuned in to her baby, she could become more sensitive to the subtle electromagnetic information encoded in the electromagnetic signals of her child; in other words the babies heartbeat was picked up in the mother's brain waves and nervous system.

*Source;* The HeartMath Institute - see 'Resources' for full article and link.

## Experiencing the energy of the heart centre with Thich Nhat Hanh

In March 2011 I met Thich Nhat Hanh, a Vietnamese Zen Buddhist monk, teacher and author. He has dedicated his life to bringing mindfulness to children and adults. The retreat was one of the most extraordinary experiences of my life.

During the retreat, he gave a talk on mindfulness in London's Trafalgar Square. Over two thousand people were present, and the noise of surrounding traffic was intensely loud. Although he had a microphone on stage, his voice was so soft that I was struggling to hear and I felt a bit frustrated!

I decided to sit calmly and accept that I couldn't hear the talk. Minutes passed, and something amazing happened. The noise of the traffic seemed to recede to the edge of the Square, and it felt as if we were contained in a massive 'bubble' of peace; I could hear every word clearly.

Many people had taken their children and babies to the talk which lasted 2 hours, yet the children were quiet throughout and all the babies slept. Later I reflected and concluded that while he was speaking, his mindful awareness of his own heart and the peace within it emanated from him in waves; his words were an extension of this heart centre energy which touched us all, young and old, in the most profound and peaceful way.

On the last day inside the retreat's auditorium, the audience waited with great excitement for Thich Nhat Hanh to give his final talk. With 350 people present, there was a lot of chatter and the energy in the room felt 'high'. We had 10 minutes to wait but I noticed that the atmosphere in the room was changing; the room became more and more quiet. The only way I can explain it is that it felt like a 'solid' feeling of silence started to extend over the room.

Next to his meditation cushion on the stage was a single rose in a vase. As I looked at the rose, I could 'see' that it was surrounded by a halo of golden light. As I looked at this in quiet disbelief, I noticed that the room itself was starting to fill with golden light. I was seeing this light as clearly as I see my own reflection in the mirror.

As I sat in wonder, I suddenly felt that he was meditating somewhere, focussing on the peace in his heart. This was expanding into the auditorium and his heart centre energy was gently connecting to all who were waiting to hear him. It was one of the most 'mind opening' moments I have ever experienced.

## An inner well of peace

I share this to help you see that when we meditate with the heart centre, we tap into a huge reservoir of peaceful energy. A heart centre meditation opens the 'door' you may have closed and allows your heart centre energy to flow far and wide. As you become aware of your heart centre intelligence, it can guide you in all your actions, words, feelings and thoughts; it can connect you to your child in a profound and beautiful way.

When we teach meditation with this heart-centred awareness, it expands and touches the energy of those around us and especially through the heart-felt words that we speak. Not only do we benefit from this experience, but it brings a calm and comforting energy to all. Children are sensitive to this and those on the autistic spectrum can really sense heart-centre energy.

## Our true 'mindful teacher' within

Part of the Connected Kids programme involves the adults practising heart centre exercises; learning to teach meditation from the heart, not the head. They touch in to their 'mindful teacher' within to deliver a bespoke meditation for that particular child or group of children. Teaching meditation in this heartfelt way is profoundly peaceful and healing for both the teacher and the child.

When you teach meditation, you may think that it is the words that will affect children, but the coherence within the heart of the meditation teacher and how this flows through the words has a powerful influence. If you practise this, you will witness what it means to teach children meditation in a heart-centred way.

For you personally, focusing on the heart centre during your own meditation practice gives you access to a 'library' of solutions that your mind can't reach on its own. To do this, you can sit in meditation, focussing on the heart and 'bridge' the energy of your heart with the mind, bringing solutions to issues that you have mindfully taken into your consciousness. Solutions arise like bubbles of air rising to the surface of water. It is a fascinating process and the more conscious you become of this inner-source, the more peaceful you'll feel. It is a wonderful practice to share with your family and others.

## Heart Centre Meditation (mindful problem solving)

You can practise this together as a group/family gathering or alone.

Give a gentle explanation to the group that this is a time to meditate on something that is a problem or causing upset. The intention to take into the meditation is to find a solution or a lesson from the perceived 'problem'.

The words in italics are a guide of what you would say to guide others or for self-practice.

*Feet on the floor or if seated on the floor, ensure your feel the ground beneath you, touching your body.*

*Let your eyes relax. Let your eyes close.*

*Notice your breath - in and out (count the breaths or follow the 'journey' of the breath in and out) - 5 to 10 breaths.*

*Keep your attention on the breath and notice how it moves in and out of your body (rise and fall of the chest).*

*Imagine you can gently let the out breath go a little longer - notice how your body responds.*

*Take your focus to the rise and fall of your chest and think of a flower sitting in the centre of your chest, as if someone had placed it there.*

*With each breath, the petals of the flower open, more and more.*

*In the centre of the flower is a golden light, like the glow of a warm flame or a star.*

*As the flower opens with each breath, the light gets bigger and brighter.*

*The light shines out of your chest - lighting up the whole chest (you can feel or see this).*

*Imagine all the answers to your problems were in this light. It is like secret library of ideas and answers.*

*Think of the problem or issue (it could be a person) and imagine it in as much detail.*

*Take that image and slide it down into your light and surround the person/issue with light.*

*It is really safe to do this - so keep breathing the energy of the problem or person into the light in your chest.*

*Imagine they start to blend with the light and disappear into it.*

*Set your intention that an answer to this person/problem will come to the surface (like water bubbles rising up). Breathe the intention into your chest/heart centre.*

*Is there a word or an image that you start to notice? Do you have a thought or a feeling? Just have an open and gentle curiosity about it.*

*Remember you can always come back to your breath if your mind becomes distracted.*

*When you are ready to finish the meditation, take your attention back the petals surrounding the light in your chest.*

*Gently come back to the breath.*

*Gently come back to your body - your feet/body touching the ground and wiggle your fingers and toes.*

*Open your eyes.*

After the meditation, try to give the group the opportunity to share by speaking, writing or drawing about what was experienced - see Chapter 14 - 'Developing emotional awareness' for more guidance on this section.

Please note that sometimes there's a helpful answer and sometimes the strong feelings just disappear - or the solution comes later.

*(As I explained in my first book, 'Calm Kids', it is more effective if you only use scripts as inspiration and try to develop your own words to help guide you and your child into meditation. If you speak from this*

*heartfelt intuition, it dramatically increases the effectiveness of the meditation).*

During our case studies, I guided Vanessa (mum of 4-year old James who had suspected Autism Spectrum Disorder and communication issues) through a five-minute heart-centred meditation as she was experiencing some difficult challenges. We practised the heart-centre approach to help her connect with James and sense what he was feeling and how she could help him. During the meditation she realised how anxious and nervous he felt all the time and that her own stress levels affected him. Vanessa decided that each day she would 'check in' with her own energy and set an intention to be calmer and more reassuring.

## Heart centre - developing meditations for children/teens

During the case studies, we worked mindfully with the heart centre to develop the most healing meditations and mindful activities that would benefit these children and their families.  This approach was so effective that it is now a key component of our Connected Kids programme.

When we teach meditation with mindfulness of the heart, it allows us to trust our instincts and respond intuitively to the needs of our children's energy.  In the Calm Kids book (and the first level of the Connected Kids programme) I teach people how to write scripts. This is not heart centered but it does help them access their creative mind.  This book (and level 2 of the programme) teaches you how to step away from written scripts or mind-based ideas; you learn to use a heart-felt inner script to find intuitive and heart-centered words and meditation ideas. The heart centre is the intuitive 'source' that provides the inspiration for the mind to translate into words and activities.

Teaching meditation this way helps us to tune into and understand children with special needs with our heart, not our minds.  It is a useful way to develop meditations when children find it difficult to communicate their needs to us. At first your logical mind may struggle to accept the flow of intuitive ideas or words and this is what I usually see happen in class. However try to let go and trust the heart; I have witnessed the powerful, healing effect this has when adults teach this way. Our Connected Kids students share their thoughts...

*"Truly is there any other way to open the treasure~box of our offerings than through the heart center? My practice reminds me that I am here as a guide so each and every child and their families may access the hidden keys within ~ nothing to teach so much as it is a reawakening of tools long lost to us."*

Kim Snyder Sterrs, USA

*"When my heart is expanded it's like we are all together in a big hug".*

Deborah Dalziel, Australia

*"When I teach from my heart, my words flow without effort, like a beautiful stream and I know that they are exactly what is needed at that moment for those who are listening. When I teach from my head, I stumble my way upstream, worrying that I will say something wrong."*

Linsey Denham, Canada

*"When I teach from the heart, I become so completely absorbed in what I am doing it is as if time becomes suspended. I feel like I am in this little bubble of calm, joy and wonder with the children. The ideas and words flow and the children's response never fails to amaze me."*

Hazel Melia, Ireland

*"When I allow the heart to talk, the energy of meditation shifts from an activity to a meaningful 'beingness' that supports the children where they are, at that very moment, perfectly. It reaches a more profound level, that enables me to plant seeds of stillness more deeply than a script and my head can ever do."*

Karen Davies, England

*"When I teach from the heart I enter a new reality; a reality that is calm, peaceful and embraces my true self. It's the real me, the essence of me, unobstructed and clear. Sometimes it doesn't last long but it's a moment of pure joy, I want all children to know that this exists."*

Jude Brown, England

*"Teaching from the heart feels like gently leading along the steps of something greater than myself."*

Helen Jacoby, Scotland

This technique is so crucial to teaching meditation that I am including an example script here.

For free access to this recording of the heart centre meditation by me, Lorraine E Murray, please visit http://www.teachchildrenmeditation.com/ to join the mailing list where you will be sent the link and the password in one of our updates.

## Heart Centre Meditation

I use this mindful practice to develop and teach all my meditations. It will help you develop your ability to follow your intuitive, heartfelt inner guidance.

*Sit in your normal meditation position (feet on the floor if seated, or connected to the ground if sitting cross-legged).*

*With hands resting in your lap and eyes closed, focus on your breath.*

*With each breath, notice the rise and fall of your chest. Do this for 5 to 10 breaths.*

*Each time you breathe out, invite your body and mind to relax and your emotions to feel calmer.*

*Take your attention to the centre of your chest and imagine a pink and golden light.*

*Imagine that the pink light is in the centre of a flower surrounded in gold and with each breath the flower opens and the light becomes brighter and stronger.*

*Sense that the light expands while filling your chest.*

*Allow it to glow more brightly with each breath.*

*Think of a child you know whom you would like to help with meditation.*

*Imagine their hair, size, height, face, eyes, their voice and their energy; in as much detail as possible, silently stating their name.*

*Take that image of them from your head and slide it down into the light in your chest.*

*Now breathe the image totally into the light, so you can imagine they are surrounded in that light.*

*Set an intention that you wish to help them with meditation, and breathe this intention into your light. Imagine the words of your intention flowing in and surrounding the child, like a blanket of love.*

*Breathe into the light in your chest for 5 more breaths until the child and the intention are one.*

*Now start to notice what ideas or thoughts you are having or any strong insights or feelings about a meditation idea or theme. Just keep breathing into the light as this develops.*

*Try not to let your analytical brain judge or question those ideas or thoughts.*

*Once you have finished (after several minutes) then let the image of the child and the intention dissolve in your heart centre 'light'*

After the meditation, write down whatever you observed.

Even if you are new to the idea of meditation, try this method. It is an excellent way to help you feel more balanced and calm, as well as giving you an intuitive way to respond to the needs of your children through meditation and any form of mindful parenting or education.

## Connecting to the heart centre - teens and children

It is equally important for you to help children tap into the intelligence of their heart centre. The following meditation will help children and teens to do this. It will help children appreciate their body, allowing them to relax and to feel physically calmer. It will also strengthen their concentration skills.

If children or teens with special needs have a tendency to fixate on the negative, this mediation is very effective at lifting them out of this downward spiral. For the parents of children with special needs, the meditation is very helpful.

If children physically smile while doing this, there will be a corresponding sensation in the physical body (usually the chest); opening the heart centre. Try it and see.

## Useful tips

The meditation is suitable for all ages of children, but you can change the length and the language depending on their attention span. If children have a short attention span, allow them to lie down to listen. Otherwise ask them to sit with their feet (or base of the spine) touching the ground.

You could ask younger children to move the relevant part of their body before they focus on it (tensing or wiggling and then relaxing).

If you are practising this with toddlers, you could ask them to touch the relevant part of their body to help with focus; they may keep their eyes open so that they can watch and copy you.

It can help to ask them to think of something that makes them feel happy and then notice where they feel that in their body. If they struggle to think of something, ask them to start by imagining a big 'smile'; asking them to notice the feeling in their body when they think about the smile. If this doesn't work, ask them to physically smile and notice where they feel that within their body (in addition to their face). You can then explain that when we silently say 'thank you' as we focus on different parts of our body, we are bringing the same feeling wherever we focus.

If your child experiences pain, you can still invite his awareness into his body encouraging him to thank the body for trying to do its best to keep everything in balance. Pain is the body's way of responding to something out of balance and if we can encourage children to say thank you to the body rather than fight it, it can help them manage their pain or discomfort.

You can combine this meditation with keeping a gratitude diary to help you and your children activate the positive energy of the heart centre. A gratitude diary is where you write down 3 to 5 things that you feel grateful for. If making a gratitude jar, you fill it up with all those moments of gratitude and it is an effective visual reminder. Children can choose to take something out of the jar and read it when they feel sad or upset.

## The 'Thank You Meditation' - opening the heart centre

*I notice my feet - I say 'thank you' to my feet. I like my feet as they help me...*
*Walk quietly in school,*
*Run with my friends in the park,*
*Skip along with friends,*
*Play my favourite games,*
*Thank you, feet.*

*I notice my legs - I say 'thank you' to my legs. I like my legs as they help me...*
*Stand without falling over,*
*Dance to my favourite music,*
*Run fast,*
*Thank you, legs.*

*I notice my tummy - I say 'thank you' to my tummy. I like my tummy as it...*
*Gives me energy to play,*
*It gurgles with lots of yummy food,*
*It helps me feel full and satisfied,*
*It supports the rest of my body,*
*Thank you, tummy.*

*I notice my lungs - I say 'thank you' to my lungs. I like my lungs as they...*
*Help me breathe,*
*I can make noises through my mouth like 'shhhhhhhhh',*
*They help me speak and say 'I love you',*
*They send air around my body,*
*They give me energy to play,*
*Thank you, lungs.*

*I notice my heart - I say 'thank you' to my heart. I like my heart as it...*
*Beats in my chest and I can feel it,*
*It helps me feel loved and give love to others,*
*It energises me and even beats when I'm asleep,*
*Thank you, heart.*

*I notice my head - I say 'thank you' to my head. I like my head as...*
*My mouth helps me to sing and talk and make silly noises,*
*My nose helps me to breathe and I can wiggle it,*
*My ears help me to hear lovely sounds like laughing and birds singing,*
*My eyes help me to see beautiful things in the world,*
*My cheeks go red when it's cold and I can puff them out like a fish,*
*Thank you, head.*

Top tips - when you begin, ask them to imagine that each 'thank you' is like a bubble or a present that they send to that part of their body.

## Centering thoughts for your personal meditation practice

How open is your heart centre?

How easy is it for you to accept/ask for help, receive a gift or a compliment?

## 7.  TUNING INTO YOUR CHILD'S ENERGY

Your child's energy is as unique as his DNA; cells in his body form muscles, bones, ligaments, organs and many other parts that we can physically identify.  We uses phrases such as "he looks like his dad", "she's got your colour of hair, eyes etc".

The energy that created him consists of the more than the physical body; you also gave him the energy of your thoughts and feelings. You inherited them from your parents, and your grandparents and your great grandparents and so on; this is our ancestral lineage of energy.

In addition to the messages our child picks up verbally and visually from the care-givers in his life, he has pre-pattered ways of thinking and feeling in situations as a result of this ancestral pattern.

Parent's often set out to be different from their own parents claiming that they'll 'never say or do that'!  But they do because playing in the background of their consciousness is the programme of the energy of all the thoughts and feelings they inherited.  One way to change this is to:

Observe

Accept

Let go

This is why your own meditation practice is just as important as the teaching practice for your children. You can consider that your children are reflecting back qualities of your energy; qualities you like and dislike about you.

It helps to be aware of this when you are teaching meditation. If they are your own children, you can work on self-compassion for these qualities you dislike within yourself. As you do, you actually help heal the energy of the ancestral lineage - both past (your relatives) and future. You free your children from repeating the same challenging lessons you have faced.

If you are working with children, you can look to the family for clues about the child's energy; fears they carry and emotions or thoughts waiting to be processed. If you tune in to the child's energy and that of the parents (using the heart centre meditation in Chapter 6 - *'Connecting to heart centre intelligence'*) you will learn how to support the child in the most healing and balanced way with mindful activities.

I teach this as part of the level 2 Connected Kids programme and have witnessed many profound healing moments for the adults training to teach meditation. Students let go of any 'ancestral baggage' which ultimately helps them and their children.

## Yin and Yang energy

We can consider a child's energy in terms of how balanced or imbalanced their chakras are (see Chapter 5 - *'Teaching meditation with energy awareness'*). However the yin/yang interpretation of energy gives us another resource that helps us tune into children's energy and their needs.

*Credit Annykos/Shutterstock.com*

The ancient Yin/Yang symbol has been used in Chinese traditions for thousands of years to demonstrate the ebb and flow of energy in our universe and especially within us and our connection to the environment.

The black energy represents the feminine, yin energy and the yang represents the male, yang energy. Both forms of energy are necessary and interact continuously to bring balance - a divine point of balance in any given moment.

The dot of the alternating colour in each part reminds us that within the yin there is yang energy and within yang there is yin.

The yin energy is the feminine, creative, spiritual, open, receptive, quiet qualities of energy. The yang is the opposite - male, logical, direct, physical, focussed, vibrant qualities of the energy. The yin is the moon, the sun is the yang.

I have very yang energy in that I can be very direct and outspoken. Learning meditation as a teenager was a powerful way for me to balance my Yang and Yin. My husband is naturally Yin but balances this with the Yang of mountain biking!

Whatever our starting point, meditation is a way to help our energy become balanced. We respond well to the mindful practice that complements our energy type. This awareness of the Yin/Yang helps us engage children in meditation.

If a child is very yang then they have a lot of energy! This is accounts for most children but some are more yin (quieter, reflective and shy).

First we tune in to our child's energy; we consider the qualities of Yin and Yang and reflect on which one they are/need help with. We intuitively choose mindful activities that suit their energy. There is little point trying to get a child who is very Yang who is constantly moving to sit still in meditation - which is why we suggest movement (like yoga) to help them focus and balance.

If a child has a lot of Yin energy, asking them to speak after a meditation would be very challenging due to their shyness. Knowing this we could offer alternative ways to express feelings and thoughts that are attuned to their current state of energy (mandalas, writing etc).

Also consider your Yin/Yang energy and how it compares to your child. Are you both very Yang? Or are you Yang and they are Yin? Understanding this can help us to develop more compassion for our children. It helps us understand that we don't connect to life in identical ways.

Here are some suggestions for introducing Yin/Yang mindful activities.

*Yang energy mindful activities* – yoga, movement but with mindful awareness (running, skipping, trampoline, labyrinth walking, meditation themes where the child's imagination uses movement – eg like a football match or swimming).

Yang energy types can have difficulty connecting to the body so using mudras, breath work with a tactile approach can help.

*Yin energy mindful activities* – sitting meditation, using word and sound meditations, mandalas, paper labyrinths, gratitude diaries or meditation themes which are about releasing difficult emotions/feelings can all help.

## The 'role' of male and female energy

Meditation has been perceived as something spiritual and emotional; the feminine. Often society suggests that connecting to feelings is more comfortable for females than men. But I've seen a change in western society with men starting to embrace the idea of meditation and yoga; allowing them to access this spiritual and emotional energy within.

This is good news, but during the case studies it was usually the female who was interested and supportive of their children learning meditation. The males seemed to be 'absent' or less interested in taking part.

I am delighted when a person is interested in teaching meditation to children but for complete balance a child needs the energy of both parents. The male energy brings a different quality to that child's life (as we have illustrated through the Yin and Yang experience).

I don't define male/female energy by gender; the yang energy is present in females and well as males (and vice versa with yin energy).

## Some personal examples:

These concepts may seem rather difficult to accept. To help, I share my own personal journey.

*My ancestral lineage*: I come from a line of strong woman, so strong that that from mother to great grandmother they all divorced their husbands and lived independently, in an era when that wasn't the 'done thing'. They also drank lots and lots of tea. My great grandmother would go to bed with a pot of tea. Although I like a cup of tea, I always felt I drank too much of it. The idea of the toxins didn't sit with my healthy lifestyle yet I couldn't stop drinking it and I would feel guilty.

One day I decided to sit down and drink a cup of tea mindfully. I brought my awareness to all the sense, smell, touch, sound, taste and sight. I observed the feeling as I drank the tea and how it travelled through my body. Then suddenly I made the connection between the tea and my family.

No-one in our family said "I love you". As a small child I was never hugged. So I realised that the cup of tea was more than this. It was a hug, it was an 'I love you' - it was the affection from my family shown in the only way they knew how to share it. Every time I had a cup of tea that brought a bit of nurture into my life. I sat with the feelings that came up from this experience and with mindful awareness, let them pass through. I no longer need to drink so much tea (and yes I do hug... often).

*Male/Female energy:* As a single parent, my mum did an amazing job. I never thought I really missed my dad (they were divorced when I was 4, I never saw him again and he died when I was 12). I thought I had managed quite well without the male influence in my life. It has taken me to the age of 45 to realise that I carried a great deal of anger towards him. I didn't know how to acknowledge this nor express it, so I pushed it down inside with addictions to work and (as a teenager) alcohol. I practised a lot of meditation, yet I noticed I would feel really angry sometimes. I would feel this river of rage rise up with certain triggers and I couldn't figure out why.

I discovered some cysts in my body and became concerned that I was holding the emotion of anger (cysts contain fluid which in energy terms relates to emotions – in this case toxins that equated to anger). So I sat in meditation with this awareness, listening to my body and noticing my thoughts and feelings. Then I realised that the anger linked to my father - it was the only emotional connection I had. If I let go of my anger, I would have no connection to him so I had held on to it.

I practised meditation to help release it and simultaneously started to build a different connection. Even though he was in spirit, I took out old photographs and visited the place where he died. Now my connection with my father, the male energy in me, is one of peace.

I share this to help you consider that a child is both male and female energy (regardless of gender). If we can consider this in child development and teaching them meditation, we can help them have balance with their feelings, energy, thoughts and challenges when a parent's energy is absent.

## Centering thoughts for your personal meditation practice

What energy have you inherited from your ancestors and what can you do to heal it?

What type of energy does your child have (yin/yang) and what mindful activity would help him feel balanced?

## PART TWO - your meditation toolkit

The following section gives you meditation 'tools' that can help children feel more connected, calmer and centred. The techniques will help all children but in my practice, I've found them to be particularly effective for children with special needs. With these simple tools and techniques we can guide them into a calmer, more peaceful place, helping them cope with challenges and release negative thoughts or anxieties.

# 8. WORKING WITH COLOUR

*"I found I could say things with color and shapes that I couldn't say any other way... things I had no words for."*

*Georgia O'Keeffe, American artist*

Using colour-based mindful activities, we can help children feel more balanced and we can use it to help them communicate and process their feelings.

Children on the autistic spectrum or with ADHD don't feel connected to their bodies like you or I. This dis-connection leaves them feeling 'ungrounded', unsafe, unbalanced and insecure which activates the stress response (fight/flight/freeze). Children don't want to feel this way; they are trying their best to live in this world, but their ungrounded energy keeps them in a constant state of stress and this makes day to day life very challenging.

We can't force children to become more grounded but we can guide them and give them tools that may help. Initially they may resist as they've become so accustomed to living in this state, but with regular practise using tools they enjoy, they can gradually bring their energy into a more grounded state. Using mindful tools that work with colour can be a positive step in this direction.

## Colour and energy

Colour is an aspect of energy. According to English physicist and mathematician, Isaac Newton, dispersion of light is when we refract the energy of light through a prism and it is split into different wavelengths (frequencies) of colour. This is how a rainbow is created in the sky. Like a rainbow, our body is a prism and as light (energy) passes through we are affected by these different wavelengths of colour within that light.

© iStock.com/setixela

Think about your favourite colour. What colour are you wearing at the moment, and what colour surrounds you? The psychology of colour has been shown to affect blood pressure and metabolism. The physical body responds to internal and external environments by adjusting and maintaining a level of homeostasis. From my experience of working with energy, we choose a colour because it balances our energy. If an energy centre (chakra) is out of balance, our energy guides us (an idea/thought/feeling) to bring it into balance using colour.

## The language of colour

Think about your child's favourite colour - what colour does he like to wear, or what is the colour of his room? He is bringing this colour into his world because energetically it helps him feel more balanced.

Colour is a way for children to express feelings that they can't articulate through words; a 'language' we can learn in order to tune in to their needs and offer support.

When our children are surrounded by their chosen colour, whether physically or in their imagination through meditation, they connect to the energy of that colour and become more balanced. Children choose the colour their energy needs intuitively rather than logically; this helps them *feel* more balanced.

Children who are ungrounded or who have ADHD often choose the colour red, brown or black, which links with the root chakra (feet, legs, base of spine and the adrenal glands).

Children with autism are drawn to purple. Purple is linked to the brow and crown chakras, and the pineal and pituitary glands are among the physical areas of the body influenced by these energy centres. We know that the pineal gland is involved in the production of melatonin (e.g. our sleep/awake cycles and sexual development) and the pituitary gland is known as the 'master gland' because of its effect on the endocrine system (glands and hormones throughout the body). Research suggests that these areas can present challenges for those on the spectrum.

## Imagining colour

We can invite a child to imagine colour and breathe it into particular parts of his body. This method is very calming and works well for children with ADHD or children with imaginations who can easily visualise a colour.

When we're teaching children on the autistic spectrum, some may struggle to 'see' colours in their imagination. One boy I worked with used coloured pencils to create different colours for his meditation; he couldn't recall the colour in his mind without having the colour pencils as a reference.

One of our Connected Kids tutors, Sheila Barnes, worked with a group of young people with learning difficulties and autism. She used a tactile approach to colour by using coloured feathers and drawings of fish. Initially, the group were unable to meditate for more than a few minutes. Within a few weeks, this extended to 25 minutes.

*"I intuitively felt a colourful, patterned feather; helping them focus on the movement of the feather. This would be a useful aid that they could keep to practise with their breath."*

Sheila Barnes, Tutor (Case Study)

If your child has difficulty visualising colour, allow him to see a range of colours before starting the meditation; he may recall colour in the short term. If he can't imagine 'feeling' colour, I suggest using a tactile approach of coloured cards or scarves that he/you can place on different parts of his body. Even though he can't see the colour, it will help him focus on his body and he can pretend that he is breathing in the colour.

Using colour in mindful activities can help children balance their energy. However we can intuitively understand issues children are feeling by the colours they choose and how it relates to the chakra system - Chapter 5 - 'Teaching meditation with energy awareness'.

## Meditation themes with colour

*The following ideas can help you use colour in mindful activities with children/teens.*

### Colour bubble

Invite your child to imagine that he is sitting in a bubble. Guide him to imagine that this bubble fills with a colour that helps him feel grounded, protected, strong, safe and happy (choose the words that *feel right* for the child you are teaching). Guide them to notice that with every breath the colour becomes brighter and stronger. Guide them to bring in the other senses (like touch) to help him feel the colour.

Tactile tip - use soapy bubbles and the act of blowing these to help his imagination.

### Colour breath

Invite your child to imagine the air around him filling with his favourite colour. Use adjectives to describe how the colour might make him feel. Ask him to imagine he is made of glass and can breathe in the colour - into his body, bones, muscles and organs which helps him relax and feel connected to his body.

Tactile tip - use a coloured balloon to help him see a colour and how the breath fills up the balloon.

### Wearing colour

Invite your child to imagine that he is wearing his favourite colour. Go through the different items he may be wearing and imagine that each of these is his favourite colour – using words that help him feel calmer, safe or strong.

Tactile tip - bring some items of clothes in his favourite colour and guide him to be aware of touch as he puts them on (this helps him to connect to his body).

### Gold and pink light

Invite your child to imagine that he is surrounded in a golden shield, making him feel totally protected and safe. He can imagine it as armour or a special cloak (if he likes superheroes then suggest something the cartoon might use? Gently ask him to think of someone who makes him feel uncomfortable - maybe it's a bully or someone he has fallen out with. This person sits outside the golden shield. Invite him to imagine that this person is surrounded with the colour pink, and wearing pink - even his hair is pink! Describe this in as much detail as possible. Explain to your child that the golden shield protects him and the colour pink changes the energy between them.

Tactile tip - use cartoons or images to help him imagine this

## Colour in guided meditations

While guiding a child in meditation, you may refer to objects and their colour - such as balloons, kites or flowers. Mentioning colour (e.g. green grass, blue sky) helps to draw a child's attention to colours that may be in the natural environment of the meditation. You can also invite him to notice how the colour makes his body feel.

Tactile tip - show him items that may appear in the meditation so he can touch/see them before meditating.

In one of our case studies, a young boy with physical disabilities was experiencing lots of anger issues. We introduced his grandmother to the idea of using a coloured balloon meditation to help him release these strong emotions - each balloon represented a negative feeling which he released into the sky.

> *"Thank you so much. Adam was violent when he got angry, but with regular meditation he has become peaceful and can sleep better. Since we started, we have taken many good things from this approach that has helped him for his mind, his behaviour and his health."*

> Barbara, Grandmother (case study)

If he cannot put his emotions into words, asking your child to choose a colour that represents how he feels is an effective way to help him process feelings and help you understand how he feels.

## Centering thought for your personal meditation practice

What is your favourite colour and how does it make you feel? Why?

# 9. MINDFUL ACTIVITIES WITH SOUND

*"If we accept that sound is vibration and we know that vibration touches every part of our physical being, then we understand that sound is heard not only through our ears but through every cell in our bodies. One reason sound heals on a physical level is because it so deeply touches and transforms us on the emotional and spiritual planes. Sound can redress imbalances on every level of physiologic functioning and can play a positive role in the treatment of virtually any medical disorder."*

*Dr. Mitchell Gaynor, Director of Medical Oncology*
*Strang Cancer Prevention Centre, New York*

Sound is created by air/water pressure that travels through the atmosphere and is perceived by a person via the physical structure in the ears where electrical signals travel via the nervous system to the brain for interpretation. Humans can hear a range of sound vibrations but sounds exist outside this and can be detected by other species (e.g; a bat using ultrasound to detect the placement of objects).

It is said that the ear starts forming a few days after conception and is fully developed by the 2nd trimester. Dr Alfred Tomatis, an internationally known otolaryngologist (ear, nose and throat physician), who developed equipment to help children and adults with a range of health issues (including autism), theorized that information coming from the foetal ear stimulates and guides the development of the brain.

From the moment babies start to register sound in the womb, they can detect the mother's heartbeat, the sound of blood moving and the mother's digestive system. The sound is not only heard, but is felt as a vibration through the baby's developing nervous system; from an early age, children are affected by sound.

## Sound and additional support needs

Certain sounds can activate the stress response in children with SPD (sensory processing disorder) where the volume or number of sounds they hear is overwhelming.

Some autistic children have a different range and relationship with sound; hearing the high pitched hum of electrical objects that *neurotypicals (you and I) are unable to detect. Hand dryers in public toilets are especially distressing for children with SPD. The intensity can initiate the stress response for these young people. We assume that children can hear and understand the sounds we make when we are speaking to them. Yet their range of sound can be different and it may be difficult for them to interpret and process (the same way we can feel when learning a foreign language). Perhaps they learn to cope by 'tuning out' the sound. To us, this appears disobedient instead of a coping mechanism.

If children grunt, hum or make a noise you don't understand, they may be doing this as the sensation and sound is a calming technique or the only way they know how to express their anxiety; consider how a dog whines (or barks) when they are anxious.

*This is a term given by the autistic community for people who are not autistic.

## Mindful awareness of sounds

When working with kids with disabilities, there are some mindful activities that can help change the connection children have with sound; their awareness of sound helps them tune into their breath and body.

We can guide a child to notice he is affected by sound and where he senses this in his body. In a sound meditation, you could guide him to feel relaxed, ask him to notice sounds he hears, where he feels the sound in his body (placing his hand there if he can) and noticing any images/thoughts/feelings that occur.

Here are a few examples of sounds you could guide your child to explore mindfully:

*Self-created sounds - giggling/laughter, sighing/yawning, humming, sounding words/vowels, singing or sounds of their footsteps. If a child is making these sounds, it will give him a connection with his body through the movement/vibration he feels.

Birdsong

Different types of music

Silence

A cat purring

The 'ping' of a message on a mobile phone

The click of the computer keyboard as he types

A clock ticking

Sounds of his footsteps on the ground

Counting sounds (number of sighs, bird tweets, heartbeat)

*You could also consider making these sounds and asking him to pay attention to his body and how it feels as he listens.

It makes sense to eliminate sounds that cause him stress, but you could invite him to *imagine* a sound he doesn't like and where he would imagine feeling this in his body. If we show our child how these sounds impact the body then we can connect the breath to the body to help him release the stress; as the physical body relaxes, it can positively impact on the mind and feelings.

Using the imagination (which can bring a physiological change to the body), try the idea of giving children a pair of imaginary, golden earphones that they use to block out sounds they find stressful. You can use the following sample to help create a meditation around this theme.

## Golden Earphones Meditation

*Invite your child to focus on his breath.*

*Guide him through his body to connect to it and relax.*

*Invite him to imagine a pair of earphones.*

*Now ask him to imagine that the earphones are 'golden' and that they will protect his ears.*

*Guide him to imagine putting the earphones on and sounds around him becoming quieter - the only thing he can hear is your voice.*

*Invite him to relax his body with each breath.*

*Ask him to imagine the golden light getting brighter and filtering out more sounds.*

*Ask him to imagine his breath slowing down - becoming calmer.*

You can suggest that he keeps wearing the imaginary earphones after the 'meditation' and he can 'activate' them when he needs to - switching on/off or changing the volume.

Some children have difficulty listening to the sound of their parent's/carer's voice. If this is the case, ask your child to imagine his favourite cartoon character and that when you speak to him that it's in the character's voice. This changes the energy between you and your child and may help them listen.

## Self-sounds

In addition to hearing sound, we make sounds when we speak. The expression of sound takes our internal world of thoughts and feelings and distributes it out into the external world. The voice is a bridge between heart and head (body and mind) and when we express who we are and are understood, we feel safe and connected. When we can't express this and feel misunderstood it makes us feel stressed and we can feel isolated.

The following suggestions are sound (and breath) mediations that can help children feel calmer when expressing sound.

## The Heart Sound Meditation

*Invite your child to place his hand on his chest (area of the heart centre).*

*Invite him to close his eyes.*

*You demonstrate first with the heart sound which is an 'aaaahhhh' that you make on the out breath.*

*Then invite him to join in.*

*As he makes the sound, guide him to feel the vibration in his chest.*

*Ask him to feel and hear the sound throughout his body.*

*Repeat the sound 3 to 10 times.*

*Then sit in silence with each other for 3 to 10 breaths.*

This is a very calming sound meditation as it connects to the heart chakra. The vibration helps your child to connect and focus on his body.

Variations of this method can include... placing your hand on his chest and his on yours as you take turns making the sound (to feel and hear it in the hand touching the chest); varying the tone and volume of the sound being made; touching the throat as he makes the sound and then the tummy to notice how the sound vibrates throughout his body.

## Ocean Breathing (also known in yoga as Ujjayi breathing)

*Invite your child to place his hand in front of his open mouth and to imagine his hand is a mirror. On each out breath, he tries to 'fog' the mirror (you can demonstrate this with a real mirror if this helps).*

*After a little bit of practice, ask him to close his mouth but still make the noise. He should be able to hear the sound of his breath - it sounds very similar to the ocean.*

*Now ask him to place his other hand behind the back of his head/top of neck and as he breathes in, he tries to make a similar noise into the back of his head where his hand touches.*

*Guide him to practise the ocean breath for approximately 10 breaths.*

*Invite him to relax and check in with his body and how it feels.*

*He can practise this breath until he reaches a point where he can let his hands rest by his sides.*

This type of breath supports concentration skills and regulates the body temperature while helping areas of tension (and the nervous system) to relax.

## Can sound harm or heal the body?

In 1999 the Japanese scholar and entrepreneur Dr Masaru Emoto published some startling photographs of water crystals. He had conducted a series of experiments in which water was exposed to a variety of sounds; music and words/phrases, both spoken and written. The water was then partially frozen and the water crystals were photographed. These images were collected over a 15 year period and the consistency in the results suggests that positive words/classical music produce different shapes compared to negative words or rock/pop music.

Beautiful, symmetrical crystals grew in a pure and peaceful environment that had positive sounds (love and gratitude - image 1); but distorted crystals formed in an environment polluted with negative sounds (you disgust me - image 2).

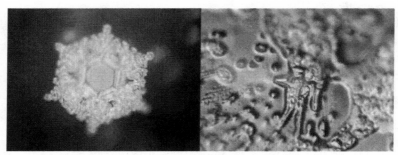

*Image 1      Image 2*
© *Office Masaru Emoto, LLC www.masaru-emoto.net*

What Dr Emoto demonstrated was the effect that a single word can have on a glass of water whether the word is spoken or written next to the water.

Since the human body is 60% to 70% water (higher in children), sound vibrations, whether transmitted by speech or music have a direct impact on the fluid within the cells of our body. If we speak angrily or negatively, we are quite literally damaging our health; but when we speak mindfully or positively, we are emitting a healing vibration. Thoughts and written words can have the same affect.

When you argue with someone; both you and the person are affected by the energy of the words. Children experience this too simply by listening to the argument.

In addition to the actual sound, the energy of the intention behind the sound can affect a child. I've spoken to many parents who often meet with resistance from their child when *asking* him to do something. Although the spoken words suggest that the child has a choice, the parent really wants a certain outcome (e.g. tries to control through the solar plexus); a child will feel and resist this. If the parent engages the heart centre before speaking, the child senses this energy and is more likely to engage.

When teaching kids meditation, try to avoid using scripts as a guide. Let your heart-led intuition affect the words you speak; your child will feel the difference and respond more positively.

## The energy behind a voice

One of our case studies was a boy called Evan who has high functioning autism and Hyperacusis (sensitivity to certain sounds).

Evan had used a sound machine for a few years prescribed for Hyperacusis which the family used every night to help him go to sleep. At the time of our case study, he had started listening to nature sounds on a phone application. His mum also tried guiding him in meditation.

> *"On the first night, I tried to lead a meditation. Evan told me to stop talking and was asleep within five minutes (this usually takes 30 minutes after reading time)."*

> Donna, Mum (case study)

Evan responded very quickly to the sound of his mum's voice (Donna had been learning and practising meditation for her own wellbeing). The energy of her relaxed state affected Evan in that he only required a short meditation to relax and go to sleep.

## Teaching children the power of silence

Adults may think that children can't cope with silence, yet I know that they do enjoy it; they simply need an opportunity to practise and guidance on how to sit with mindfulness.

We fill their worlds with the sound of our voices just as we pack in too many activities for them to do each day, then we wonder why they can't 'switch off'!

We can teach children to develop an awareness of sound and silence, offering children the opportunity to connect to their breath and body - balancing their energy.

## Singing bowls

A singing bowl (as shown below) is a type of standing bell, often used by Eastern cultures to mark the start and end of a meditation or it can become a sound meditation.

During the 1960s, biophysicist Erwin Neher researched brain waves created in a meditative state using an EEG (electroencephalogram which measures the electrical activity of the brain). He discovered that brain waves produced during a meditative state created by singing bowls are found to be exactly like those of alpha waves which are the relaxed-alert stage found in meditation states. The alpha state is also the stage before we enter deeper consciousness/sleep states of theta and delta brain waves (which I discuss in more detail in 'Calm Kids').

*Source:* Neher, A. (1961). Auditory driving observed with electrodes in normal subjects. Electroencephalography and Clinical Neurophysiology, 13, 449-451

*Credit: Alltogether Kids*

If singing bowls can produce this relaxed state, then they become a useful tool for teaching meditation. Playing these sounds usually helps to bring children's energy centres into balance. Just allowing children to listen to the sound can be deeply relaxing. They can be very effective with children on the autistic spectrum.

(Most children enjoy the sound of the singing bowls but <u>very</u> occasionally they don't! It is best to download a recording to test the response before purchasing a singing bowl.)

> *"We use the singing bowl often at bedtime now and it was delightful to see my son ask both his big sisters if he could do it with them. He went through the whole meditation adding in some lovely extra bits of his own - that the "energy of our meditations*

101

*was in the bowl now so when they invited it to sing the lovely calm energy of mum and me are in there". Wonderful!"*

Andrea Duffin, Connected Kids Tutor

## Meditation ideas with a singing bowl

### Following the sound

Singing bowls are useful meditation tools for focus and concentration. Hold the bowl in one hand, palm open. Tap the bowl once with the mallet to make the sound. Ask your child to listen (eyes closed) while 'following' the sound. You could ask younger children to raise their hand when they can't hear it any more. This will help improve focus and attention.

### Feeling sounds

When you tap the singing bowl, ask your child to feel the sound in his body. Where does his body tingle or twitch? Ask him to breathe in the sound as he listens and tunes in, to notice how the sound makes him feel. This is a good way to help children connect to the body.

### Inviting the singing bowl to 'sing'

The singing bowl sits on the floor or cushion. Invite your child to acknowledge the bowl (hands together at his chest, palms touching and bowing to the bowl just as if were a person). Your child sets a loving intention (e.g. "I want everyone who hears this bowl to feel happy"). Then he holds the bowl on the palm of one hand (if it is too big it can rest on the floor), focuses on his breath, relaxes his body, and as he breathes out he taps the bowl, inviting it to sing. If in a group, the children all listen to the sound to help their focus and concentration. If the child who taps the bowl is holding it in his hand, ask him to both listen and feel the sound, as it will be vibrating in his hand; this is helpful with children who have a hearing impairment. In a group, you may wish to alternate who invites the bowl to sing at the beginning and end of the meditation session.

## Helping the bowl to sing

Place the singing bowl on the floor or on the child's hand and run the mallet gently around the edge of the singing bowl (as shown in the above photo). Guide your child through the steps above (acknowledging, intention, breath, body, relax). Then show him how to let the mallet move around the edge of the singing bowl. As he does this, it's important to guide him to relax, focus on his breath and keep his hands relaxed (especially his hand holding the mallet). This mindfulness activity requires focussed concentration and works well with teenagers too.

## Tuning forks

I discovered tuning forks through a workshop with sound expert Jonathan Goldman. In one session it released chronic pain I held in the right side of my body. There is a 'tuning fork mindful activity' (below) based on this experience and which can encourage a cross connection between the right and left hemispheres of the brain.

Sound therapist Bridget Mary-Clare told me about an experience she had while working with a young boy with ADS (Attention Deficit Syndrome):

*"I work with Sound Therapy and one day a stressed mother contacted me regarding her 13-year-old son. In her words, he had been diagnosed as suffering from ADS; she had learned certain routines for helping to calm him when extremely agitated, but nothing really helped his mind. The boy was very keen to come and talk to me about his struggle.*

*I demonstrated how to sound three particular tuning forks to create relaxation, then allowed him to trust his own instincts. I noticed that he became very still, taking deeper breaths and we sat together in silence for probably three or four minutes until he lifted his head, looked me directly in the eyes and said, "This is the first time I have ever been able to stop my thoughts and be quiet."*

*He then selected another tuning fork and I explained how to apply it and he said, "This is the sound of the earth and this is the sound I have heard in my head for a long time but now I know what it is.*

*He then played with that fork, quietly stroking it around his body whilst relaxing. Finally I demonstrated some simple relaxation techniques which his mother could use, particularly when settling him for sleep.*

*I am sure the tuning forks can make a contribution in this field of work in helping parents and carers as well as their children."*

Bridget Mary-Clare, Sound Therapist
Re-creation Foundation

(The image here is of a pair of tuning forks; one for note C at 256Hz and one for note G at 384Hz which are available to buy from Jonathan Goldman - see Resources for more information).

## Tuning Forks - Mindful Activity

*Hold the long tuning fork (note G) in the right hand and the shorter one (note C) in the left hand and stand behind your child.*

*Strike the forks of your knees or a table then hold either side of your child's head (note G at the right ear and note C at the left ear).*

*Ensure that the tuning forks sound is not dulled by touching the head/hair.*

*Invite your child to close his eyes and listen and breathe in the sound.*

*Then start again, repeat the striking of the forks and cross hands so that they are held to the opposite ears.*

*Your child listens with eyes closed and listens and breathes in the sound.*

*Keep repeating the above steps for up to 10 times.*

This exercise seems to create a feeling of relaxation of the physical body and a sense of calmness. If you demonstrate the activity, older children can practise it by themselves.

**If your child experiences seizures, <u>please consult a sound therapist</u> before trying this exercise.**

## The benefits of self-created sound

I am grateful to Jonathan Goldman for the following written especially for 'Connected Kids':

> *"Sound can do extraordinary things - especially self-created sound. When I first began my work with sound, I focused on the use of vocal harmonics - a specific way of working with elongated vowels and other sounds to produce two audible notes at the same time. I was extremely interested in whether or not these sounds could be used to create new neural synaptic connections in the brain.*
>
> *While I have not yet had the opportunity to research this, it is my understanding that this ability to create new neural synaptic connections is quite possible. In fact, I believe there are extraordinary healing possibilities with the use of vocal harmonics and other self-created sounds as a means of stimulating different portions of the brain.*
>
> *As we learn more and more about the neuroplasticity of the brain, I am sure we will find that our own self-created sounds can truly contribute to the flexibility and healing of the brain. We will find that many different conditions can benefit through our working with self-created sounds.*
>
> *As I continue teaching the use of sound as a means of healing and transformation, I find that more and more of those benefits of sound, which I speculated upon over 25 years ago, have now been proven. While my initial interest in sound was primarily in vocal harmonics, which was the main subject of my first book, 'Healing Sounds', I've now found that it is not necessary for a person to become adept at producing vocal harmonics in order to receive the therapeutic benefits of self-created sounds.*

Colleagues such as Dr. Ranjie Singh of Canada, author of 'Powerful Self-healing Techniques' and Dr. John Beaulieu, of New York, author of 'Human Tuning', among many others, have researched the effects of self-created sound and found that powerful molecules and hormones are produced when we make our own sound. It is as though we are giving ourselves an internal massage that has very powerful benefits.

Our voice has amazing abilities to create shift and change within ourselves. We do not need to be trained singers to receive the extraordinary results of self-created sound. Just humming or sounding elongated vowels will produce these effects. As noted in my book 'The Divine Name', some of the scientific data on the beneficial physiological effect of self-created are:

- *Increased oxygen in the cells*

- *Lowered blood pressure and heart rate*

- *Increased lymphatic circulation*

- *Increased levels of melatonin - a hormone that helps regulate sleep*

- *Reduced levels of stress-related hormones such as cortisol*

- *Release of endorphins - self-created opiates that work as 'natural pain relievers'*

- *Boosted production of interleukin-l, a protein associated with blood and planet production*

- *Increased levels of nitric oxide (NO), a molecule that is a vascular dilator associated with promotion of healing*

- *Release of oxytocin, the 'trust' hormone*

Jonathan Goldman, Author of 'The 7 Secrets of Sound Healing', www.healingsounds.com

## Singing the vowels

Each chakra has an associated tone and a sound. Singing the vowels is a great way to help balance the energy centres, and it allows children who struggle with self control, to combine mindfulness with sound. I was inspired to try this technique in my classes after meeting Jonathan.

I appreciate that there are many mantras (sacred words) that people chant in meditation however this is not always appropriate for certain teaching environments. Teaching children to make sounds based on the vowels offers a secular approach.

## Creating Sound Meditation

Guidelines: Starting at the root chakra, work your way up to the crown. Afterwards, bring the focus back down to the root to make sure your child's energy is grounded. To encourage mindfulness, ask him how it felt in his body as he was making that sound. Invite him to notice his thoughts and feelings in the moments of silence.

*Your child can be seated or lying down (for kids with longer attention spans, encourage them to sit).*

*To begin, you make the sound and then invite him to join in. Encourage your child to let the sound flow through him rather than trying to 'make' the sound with effort and will.*

*For each vowel (below), make a sound on the out-breath (and repeat the sound for 3 breaths). After making the sound, sit in silence for 3 breaths and guide your child to notice his body and how it feels.*

*Ask him to feel the vibration move through his body as he makes the sound; noticing how tense or relaxed his body (particularly around the mouth and the tummy).*

*Focus on the base of the spine - imagine a red ball of light or spotlight. Breathe in and then out. On the out-breath, make the sound 'UUUUrrrrrrgggghhhhh' as low as you can.*

*Focus on the belly button - imagine an orange ball of light or spotlight. Breathe in and then out, making the sound 'ooooooo'.*

*Focus on the solar plexus (in the centre, above the tummy and below the chest) - imagine a yellow ball of light or spotlight. Breathe in and then out, making the sound 'awwwww'.*

*Focus on the chest - imagine a pink or green ball of light or spotlight. Breathe in and then out, making the sound 'aaaaahhh'.*

*Focus on the throat - imagine a blue ball of light or spotlight. Breathe in and then out, making the sound 'aaaaayyyyyyeeee'.*

*Focus on the brow - imagine a purple ball of light or spotlight. Breathe in and then out, making the sound 'haaaaaayyyyyyy'.*

*Focus on the crown - imagine a ball of white light or spotlight. Breathe in and then out, making the sound 'eeeeeeeeee'.*

Another option is to ask children to imagine flowers or a coloured shape instead of the light. Or if your child can't imagine any of this, ask him to think about the relevant part of his body. Some children may relax more if they can put their hand on the relevant part of their body as they make the noise, feeling the vibration of sound in their hand. Or you can place a small beanbag on each chakra point.

The sound can go up or down the musical scale - it doesn't have to be exact! Let children make the sounds they enjoy. The tone for the root is usually quite deep and the crown is usually quite high. Children can practise the sound for one to seven times; longer repetitions require the child to have more focus. I usually teach children to match one breath of silence to each sound they make (so if we sit for 3 sounds then we sit in silence for 3 breaths). Remember... giggling is allowed! This is also sound (and it releases endorphins into the blood stream helping children to release stress).

The 'creating sound' meditation can help a child feel calmer before trying a guided meditation journey or simply used as a meditation in its own right. It is useful for children who find it difficult to listen or talk.


Jaden was seeing a therapist for Obsessive Compulsive Disorder. As his mum, Renee, started to teach him sound meditations by chanting 'Om' and listening to sounds in nature, she noticed some positive progress.

*"He shocked me again last night when he was tired and throwing a big tantrum in the car and then suddenly chose to turn it off. This was not accessible to him in the past—if he got caught up in a tantrum it would have lasted for hours and hours."*

Renee, Mum (case study)

## Singing songs with children

Younger children can learn meditation in a number of ways. Children can enjoy mindful singing, and it has several benefits such as:

- massaging their internal organs with sound;

- making the vowel sounds in song which will positively affect their energy centres;

- it introduces them to mindfulness through song.

I love this mindful approach to singing (for children and adults), from the Plum Village Monastery. I learned the 'happiness is here and now' song on a retreat with the monastery founder, Thich Nhat Hanh, in 2012 and find that it has a gentle and soothing quality.

https://www.youtube.com/watch?v=BD58WmrRhdE

*(The lyrics are available in the book 'Planting Seeds: Practising Mindfulness with Children' by Thich Nhat Hanh - see Resources.)*

## Centering thought for your personal meditation practice

How do feel about the sound of your own voice? Do you feel heard?

# 10. MANDALA MEDITATIONS FOR HEALING AND BALANCE

*"I used a mandala with a little boy aged 8 with severe dyslexia. It worked very well. According to his teacher he struggles to remain on task and complete his work. However, when I gave him a mandala to work with he really took to it. He became completely absorbed in it and stayed with it until he had finished it to his satisfaction. His parents were amazed! It was wonderful to see!"*

*Hazel Melia, Connected Kids Tutor*

*Credit: Mandala courtesy of Thaneeya McArdle*

The word 'mandala' means 'circle' and it originates from an ancient language called Sanksrit.  It is often applied as a meditation practice to express creativity while helping with focus and concentration. Many children and adults enjoy the healing experience of a mandala meditation.

*"The mandala is representative of the spiralling, cyclical nature of creation. At the centre of all mandalas, there exists a key to the powerful point of stillness. Working with the many variations of this ancient form can improve focus and awareness.*

*"Round and Round the Garden', like many other games based on circles and spirals that children create, enables them to access that point of stillness."*

Liz Bell, Grandmother and Therapist

## An expression of energy

On one level, creating or colouring a mandala may seem to be nothing more than a simple drawing or colouring exercise. Since the first publication of this book, adult colouring books have become popular as a calming method for reducing stress. Mandala meditations help children and young people process difficult thoughts and feelings in a more peaceful way.

When a child colours a mandala, the colours he chooses and the way he colours the mandala becomes a representation of his energy, his feelings and thoughts... in that moment. As mandalas contain many shapes and patterns, the mandala can be a mindful meditation tool to help your child release thoughts and emotions into the picture. This may happen naturally when we draw, yet we don't notice it unless we are trained to do so.

*Credit: Yo-yo Yoga*

*"Mandalas show up in many ancient carvings and images around the world. Although mandalas came from ancient Eastern*

*practices and religions, it's believed that the modern day use of mandalas was introduced to Western culture by the renowned psychiatrist Carl Jung.*

*He noticed that he had a desire to create mandalas during periods of personal growth and that they often reflected what was going on with him at that point in time. Psychologist David Fontana also believes that meditating with mandalas works at a far deeper level of our subconscious."*

Lesley Brannen, Therapist and Mum of autistic son

## A healing meditation

The act of colouring in a mandala is a healing meditation. It helps our children to focus and improve concentration, and it is an effective way for all ages to practise mindful awareness of their breath, body, thoughts and emotions. It is an opportunity for children to express their creativity through the colours they choose as well as what they choose to colour within the mandala (creating their unique design).

Mandalas can activate creativity and healing for adults who use it as a mindful activity . The effect is greater if you use your non-dominant hand.  Using your dominant hand activates one side of the brain.  Using your non-dominant hand activates both parts of the brain, allowing brain hemispheres to connect.  Studies in the University of New South Wales by Dr Thoman Denson have suggested that using our non-dominant hand increases our ability to self-control and reduce aggression.

We must be mindful not to force children to use their non-dominant hand (in the past left-handed children were forced to use their right hands at school).  If we gently encourage children with ADHD to colour a mandala with their non-dominant hand (or switch between the 2 hands) this could help them develop self-control.

Mandalas can also help us connect to our children through the colours they choose. Each chakra has a corresponding colour, so the colours have a symbolic meaning and can tell us more about their energy centres and which ones are being balanced through the mandala.

Many feelings and emotions can be processed while completing a mandala. Your child's can be guided to notice how the mandala makes them feel and whether to keep or release it. Keeping it can become a reminder of those positive feelings. The child can release the negative feelings by destroying the mandala. This symbolic act helps to release that energy.

(For more information on mandalas and how to source them, please see 'Resources').

## Sharing the experience

It is important for you and your child to each colour your own mandala. The shared experience gives you more empathy and compassion for your child, and it demonstrates your personal commitment to meditation.

When teaching, I ask adults to practise the same mindfulness activities that they're teaching to children, this includes mandalas. I invite them to use their non-dominant hand to help them practise mindfulness.

It is always interesting to see the unique effect that mandalas have on people. For one mother, the frustration brought a sudden and profound understanding of the struggles her son had faced.

> *"When I was on the Connected Kids course, we got the opportunity to try a mindful activity of colouring in mandalas. "Excellent," I thought, "I've always loved a bit of colouring in!" I thought it would be quite a restful and peaceful meditation.*

*We were then asked to use the pen with our non-dominant hand. I could feel my frustration and unease at this request. I found it hard to control the pen, and all I could think about was how difficult it was to colour in as well as I would have liked.*

*As I focused mindfully on this sense of frustration, I was overcome with emotion as I realised that this was exactly how my nine-year-old son with dyspraxia has felt when he was asked to write. He had always struggled with writing and it obviously caused him deep anxiety. Even though I have tried to understand, it was hard for me to see how it wasn't an easier task for him. He would bring home sheets and sheets of writing from school that he hadn't finished in class, and he would be in tears as we tried to get through it for the next day.*

*As I was using my non-dominant hand, I realised that this was how my son felt as he was trying to write with his dominant hand. Difficulty controlling the pen, frustration at not having the dexterity to make it go in the direction that would be best, tired and sore hand muscles, but most of all a knot in my stomach meant that this was not by any means a relaxing meditation.*

*It was like a 'light bulb moment' for me.*

*My son is now home-schooled and does all his work on a computer. Now, as the stress from writing has been taken away, he will willingly pick up a pen or pencil for enjoyment with no expectations of how his handwriting should be. He is free to type or talk about what is in his mind, rather than focusing entirely on how good his handwriting is. It's as if the release of stress... has connected him to the freedom of his imagination and peace."*

Andrea Duffin, Connected Kids Tutor

## How can a mandala help children who have special needs, autism or ADHD?

*Focus and concentration*

Mandalas can help children focus and concentrate. You may find that, initially, your child doesn't stay within the lines, or doesn't complete the mandala. Don't be disheartened. I've often started a mandala and not 'finished' it, yet for me it was complete. Remember, every experience of meditation is an expression of our energy. There are no right or wrong answers in meditation, just the experience of the journey.

*Motor skills*

A mandala is a great way to help children develop their fine motor skills while using coloured pens or pencils. There are no 'rules' - let them know that they can do whatever they wish. Ask your child which hand he wishes to colour with: you may be surprised to find it is not always his dominant hand.

*Awareness*

Completing a mandala doesn't seem like a meditation, but it is! This is a great way to create a meditation 'game' where children do what seems like a natural activity but you guide them to be mindful. When I'm guiding someone to colour a mandala, I usually ask them to focus on their breath and be aware of how their body feels and what they are feeling inside. You are not asking them to tell you how they feel, but just for them to notice it, then let it go with each breath.

*Creativity*

You could present your child with circle and encourage him to design his own mandala. Ask him to use the shape as a starting point and to develop a design. This may be an interesting way to engage a child with autism, as it provides him with structure, yet there is also the opportunity for creativity - balancing logic with imagination.

*Use of colour*

Mandalas bring the energy of colour into our meditation, and the colours that children choose can reflect their feelings and energy. By encouraging them to use colour, we are supporting the right side of their brain, which connects with their imagination; this is helpful if they are non-imaginative or find it difficult to imagine colour.

> *"It's a quiet and calming activity that my daughter (on the autism spectrum) will often go to now when she is feeling out of control in her body.*
>
> *I will sit quietly next to her and color my own as well (if the situation and time permits). I find it calming and centering as well and I feel I'm better able to help her and she's better able to communicate her needs with me after we take a little time to color (even after just a few minutes, I find that she is better able to access "her words" to articulate what she needs) and I feel calm and centered and much more accessible to her at that point.*
>
> *We also have used them as part of our daily mindfulness practice when time allows.....if we have extra time, I give her a choice of centering activities and she will often pick mandalas.*

> Beth Studdiford

## Before beginning a mandala...

Here are some mindful guidelines when teaching mandala meditations:

- Ask your child to focus on his breath and his body to relax.

- Give him different mandala designs to choose from.

- Invite him to set an intention, such as how he wants to feel. For example, a child may want to feel happy (positive), or release worrying thoughts about a school bully (negative).

- Invite him to mindfully choose the colours he wishes to use.

- Invite him to notice where he wants to start colouring.

- Guide him to notice his breath, his feelings, thoughts and his body as he colours.

- Repeat some of these comments intermittently to help him remain mindful but give him time to enjoy drawing and colouring the mandala.

- Don't over-analyse what your children choose to do. Just have a gentle, intuitive curiosity and awareness of what is happening. Remember that a mandala isn't necessarily finished in one 'sitting' - it can take many months for it to be complete.

A great sense of liberation and freedom comes from working with a mandala. This is why it is such a powerful meditation tool.

If you or your child finds that strong and difficult feelings come up when colouring the mandala, you can choose to destroy it. The mandala holds the energy of the emotions and thoughts that were processed as it was completed; releasing it will transform this energy.

## Meditating with a mandala

If your child is happy to keep the mandala, and perhaps hang it on his bedroom wall, it can become a meditation tool. The energy of the colours will continue to help him process the thoughts and feelings that came up.

We all have thoughts and feelings about our environment, continuously (though somewhat subliminally). Consider items in your home and whether you have a memory associated with them - how you came to have them - perhaps they were a gift, or you bought them on holiday, or you simply decided to treat yourself. That item can provoke much thought and emotion if we become mindful of it. The same is true of the mandala.

*"I have incorporated mandalas into a mindfulness space in our house; it's a quiet and calming activity that my daughter (on the autism spectrum) will often go to when she is feeling out of control in her body. I will sit quietly next to her and colour my own too. I find it calming and centering and I feel I'm more able to help her. She's better able to communicate her needs with me after we take a little time to colour; even after just a few minutes, I find that she is better able to access "her words" to articulate what she needs. We occasionally use them as part of our daily mindfulness practice. I give her a choice of centering activities and she will often pick mandalas."*

Beth Studdiford, Connected Kids Tutor

Here are some suggestions on how you might guide your child to meditate with a mandala.

## Mandala Meditations

### Mandala - No. 1

*Ask your child to sit with the mandala where he can see it.*

*Guide him to focus on the mandala. As he does this, ask him to notice his breath and his body, in particular any sensations he may feel, and where they are in his body.*

*Ask him to breathe the image of the mandala into that part of his body. In doing this, he may be working with a chakra - you can both review this after the meditation. Continue this for a few moments. If he can't tell you, ask him to guess. If that doesn't work, just ask him to breathe it into his chest (the heart centre).*

*Now, if he wishes, he can close his eyes and imagine the mandala in that part of his body; breathing in the colours until eventually he imagines that he is inside the mandala, or that he is the mandala.*

*You can ask him to imagine the mandala expanding and perhaps absorbing certain thoughts and feelings.*

*Guide him to focus on his breath again and again (when we focus on the breath, it helps us feel safe). If he needs help to do this, ask him to place a hand on his chest or tummy, so that he can feel the breath.*

*Allow the meditation to continue for as long as your child is comfortable focusing; it may be one to ten minutes, or longer. You can also guide your child to flow with the energy of the mandala into a guided journey to a happy place of his choice. When you are ready to guide him back, he can imagine the mandala dissolving as he comes back to his breath and his body.*

Mandala No. 2

*Ask your child to place the mandala underneath him.*

*Guide him to focus on his breath. Use a word to help him focus; some suggestions are 'happy', 'calm', 'peace', 'fun', 'play', or 'joy'. He simply thinks about the word and imagines breathing the word in and out.*

## Non-paper mandalas

If you have a garden or open space where the mandala won't be disturbed, you could let your child create his own mandala with stones, shells, twigs, flowers, crystals or draw on paving stones with chalk!

*Credit: Pink and Green*

Creating the design is the first part of the meditation; to begin you would draw a circle. The experience will help your child come into contact with the Earth, so it is very grounding.

Later, there is the option to release the mandala. Light a small bonfire, and throw the different parts of the mandala onto it; or you could give your child a broom to sweep the mandala away. Some of the natural elements will go back to the earth. If you used crystals, these could be cleansed under water.

Buddhists create mandalas from coloured sand on a board. This is another idea to try with children. When it is finished, the mandala is offered up to the elements for the wind to blow it away. This allows the energy of the mandala to be grounded, returning it to the earth to be recycled and transformed.

Here is a crystal mandala idea from therapist Liz Bell.

## Crystal Mandala Mindful Activity

*Placing crystals within a mandala brings in their vibrational energy and healing properties.*

*Provide your child with a small bowl of crystals: rose quartz for comfort and love; blue lace agate for vocal and auditory understanding; carnelian to calm butterflies in the stomach (fear-based emotions); red ruby to cocoon in a blanket of security and grounding energy; or indeed any crystal that you or your child feels particularly drawn to.*

*The idea is that your child places as many of the crystals as he wishes into the mandala, and you create your meditation based on his choice of crystals and the picture that the mandala, as a whole, presents. Your child doesn't need to be told the properties of each crystal; he will intuitively choose the crystals that reflect his inner world at any given time.*

*The mandala can remain in place for as long as your child wishes, and he can change the crystals to reflect his feelings at any time. This enables him to connect with the positive energy of the mandala by focusing on it at any time in his day. As the mandala evolves to reflect his inner world, it can be used as a point of focus for meditation, and indeed for any time of inner reflection or relaxation.*

*Credit: Liz Bell*

*"I have a little one who is on the autistic spectrum. He struggles to focus on any one thing for more than 10mins. However, he will sit completely content and focused with a mandala for 30 minutes or more and is always keen to go back to finish. I would not do a meditation session without one!"*

While mandalas are a meditation tool, they can be used after another mindful activity (guided meditation, yoga etc.) Sometimes children find it easier to express their feelings in a mandala rather than speak about it face to face. We explore this further in Chapter 14 - *'Developing emotional awareness'.*

## Centering thought for your personal meditation practice

How does the idea of using a mandala for personal and teaching meditation practice make you feel? Are there any sensations in your body?

## 11. BALANCING THE BRAIN WITH LABYRINTHS

*"People usually consider walking on water or in thin air a miracle. But I think the real miracle is not to walk either on water or in thin air, but to walk on earth. Every day we are engaged in a miracle which we don't even recognize: a blue sky, white clouds, green leaves, the black, curious eyes of a child—our own two eyes. All is a miracle."*

*Thich Nhat Hanh, Author and Teacher*

Labyrinths are an exceptional tool to help teach children meditation, especially those with special needs.

They have a circular design like the one shown here; a single, non-branching path leads to the centre.  If you think it's a maze, it isn't.  A labyrinth has one way in (to the centre) and one way out so there is no danger of becoming stuck or lost.

*© Connected Kids Ltd*

This photo shows a vertical labyrinth for finger tracing; it is placed next to a 'walking' labyrinth on the ground.  The labyrinth encourages you and your child to practise walking meditations; mindful of the breath, body and the senses.  For young people, it can engage their interest in a walking meditation practice while bringing a balancing effect to the brain.

Di Williams, an Anglican priest and founder of Still Paths, a UK-based labyrinth resource and consultancy, gives us further insights:

> *"Walking the archetypal pattern of the labyrinth, particularly the medieval design with its many left and right turns, allows the walker a simple, safe, bounded path to bodily wander step by step. With the left brain engaged in focusing on the path and its turns, the right brain is freed up to engage with the intuitive and creative. The physical rebalancing of walking the turning places along the path thus works unconsciously on the whole brain to help unknot the old patterns of behaviour and free up new and often healing possibilities of inner connecting, thinking and feeling. As someone once said... the body has the wisdom to know how to balance itself."*

## Benefits of a Labyrinth Meditation

The labyrinth meditation can help to quieten the chatter of your child's mind as it helps connect the left and right hemispheres of the brain. As he moves along the path he learns to focus and it helps ground his energy. Depending on his attention span and age, he can use it to reflect on problems and solutions. If your child prefers movement to sitting, walking a labyrinth can be an effective meditation tool.

Balancing the hemispheres of the brain, as described by Di Williams, helps the neurological development of your child's brain.

> *"We live in an increasingly fast-paced culture in which many children and young people experience difficulty in dealing with the often stressful expectations that arise from their daily experience of home, school and community life. It can be easy to lose a sense of inner balance, to feel out of kilter with the world and with themselves. Labyrinths appear to offer a way of slowing*

*down, quietening the busy mind and rediscovering a greater sense of inner balance and rest.[1]"*

[1] (For 30 years, Herbert Benson at Harvard University has championed the physiological benefits of meditation, which he calls the 'relaxation response'. He recognises that meditation slows breathing, heart, and metabolic rates, and lowers elevated blood pressure. As a form of walking meditation, the labyrinth produces the same results.) Facilitators Digest, Vol 54, Issue 12 www.veriditas.org

## How to walk a labyrinth

Usually, a labyrinth is laid out on the ground, so that your child can walk it mindfully. The entrance and exit points are the same. This frees your child to follow the path without pressure. He can choose to take a breath before he changes direction, to focus on his breath/senses as he walks or become aware of his thoughts and feelings.

On entering, the intention is to encourage your child to walk mindfully. Don't despair if this doesn't happen. Di Williams assured me that children will interact with the labyrinth in the way that feels right for them; we can guide them to use it but we shouldn't control their steps.

Once your child is in the centre of the labyrinth, you can guide him to notice how he feels - his thoughts, senses and the breath - before making the return journey.

*© Andrew Guthrie*

## Labyrinth guidelines

- Invite your child to set an intention before entering the labyrinth - e.g, to feel 'happy' or 'peaceful'. He could think about a problem and intend that the labyrinth walk will help him release it.

- There isn't a 'right' way to walk a labyrinth. As with all meditation the journey is a unique experience for all.

- From time to time, encourage your child to notice feelings, thoughts and his body (you may wish to ring a singing bowl or bell to help them stop and connect to this).

- If he is walking with others, show him how to be respectful of the walking pace of others.

- He can walk in socks or even barefoot (very grounding).

- He can walk slowly or quickly, sing, dance or skip his way through the labyrinth!

- He can intend that, when he reaches the centre, he will feel or receive something - perhaps an answer to a question - or leave something there that he no longer needs (so you could guide him to notice his thoughts, feelings and how his body is responding in each moment of his breath - invite him to close his eyes.

I urge you, as the adult, to join in as this will encourage your child to take part and perhaps follow your actions as guidance.

## Labyrinths - young people with special needs

A parent who attended our 'Connected Kids' course took her son to a labyrinth for a walking meditation. Her son, who has high functioning autism, finds it difficult to sit still. He moves quickly, finding it challenging to relax. She wasn't confident that it would work. She planned to walk it too but her son had a habit of running away and she imagined she might have to abandon her mindful walk and give chase.

At first, she was disappointed to notice that her son walked the labyrinth quickly and didn't seem particularly mindful, but she tried to release her expectations. Then her son surprised her. When he reached the centre, he chose to walk backwards on his 'outward' journey which naturally slowed his pace, helping him be more mindful.

The biggest result was his patience; although he finished it before her, he waited outside for her to finish. Something in his energy had changed as he seemed more grounded and balanced.

The movement through a labyrinth seems to help the two cerebral hemispheres in the brain have a more balanced connection. The physical movement of the body and the movement of the eyes as they look in different directions will engage different parts of the brain. The logical, thinking part of the brain 'knows' that there is one way in and one way out so can take a rest, yet the creative brain is engaged as the path twists and turns towards the centre.

> *"I have used giant sized floor labyrinths with children with special needs. Some find it quite difficult and some remember every single step having just done it once. I could take the maze out 6 months later and these kids will remember the steps like as if they were on them yesterday. But all of them concentrate really well and are very much in the moment doing it."*

> Nicola Foxe, Connected Kids Tutor

## Creating your own labyrinth

If you don't live near a labyrinth, you can create one on a smaller scale. A labyrinth can be drawn on paper using a single line or a series of circles and shapes. You can find copies of labyrinths for children on the internet. Your child can follow the pattern of the labyrinth with a pen, a pencil, or his fingertip. Ask him to keep his pen or finger in contact with the paper all the time, as if it were walking the labyrinth. Start from the outside, and when he reaches the centre he can retrace his path back to the start.

I have discovered a hand held wooden version from Pilgrim Paths that provides an alternative labyrinth meditation. This would work well for children with a visual impairment or who find it difficult to walk.

> *"A teacher here in the U.S. contacted me last fall to tell me she was using pages from my labyrinth book with her special needs students for meditation/relaxation during the school day. She found it very effective.*

Aliyah Schick,
Author of the '*Labyrinths Meditative Coloring Book*'

*Credit: Labyrinths Meditative Coloring Book, by artist/author Aliyah Schick*

If you would like to create a walking meditation, you can create a labyrinth out of twigs, stones, shells or crystals or it could be drawn with chalk on paving stones. The act of creating a labyrinth becomes a moving meditation in itself, with lots of grounding energy!

## Centering thought for your personal meditation practice

What issues/feelings would you like to release into a labyrinth meditation?

What insights would you like to receive?

# 12. CALMING THE NERVOUS SYSTEM

*"Autism is a neurological disorder. It's not caused by bad parenting. It's caused by abnormal development in the brain. The emotional circuits in the brain are abnormal and there are differences in the white matter, which is the brain's computer cables that hook up the different brain departments."*

*Temple Grandin, Biologist, Author and Educator*

Temple Grandin talks about abnormal brain development but I prefer the term 'neurodiversity' as it can help us understand that children with dyspraxia or autism have brains that are simply wired differently from you and I. Neurodiversity suggests that this is a natural human variation rather than a disorder or pathology; that children with autism simply have a different response to the world. When we teach children mindful activities, we are giving them life skills to adapt and cope.

## The stress response - children on the autistic spectrum

Take a moment to consider that perhaps a child on spectrum experiences a constant level of stress. They struggle to filter out sound, light, touch, taste or smell so they feel constantly bombarded with information and their bodies interpret this as a threat. In this state, your child can experience a range of symptoms such as muscle tension, digestive issues, sleep problems, physical and mental tiredness, anxiety and sweating; he can easily over-react to situations, sometimes with aggression.

In addition to being overwhelmed externally, there can be an internal overload. The chemicals and toxins in his food have a powerful effect on the digestive and urinary systems of his body. Perhaps he has intolerance to wheat, gluten or sugar which are a heavy part of western diets. His body has to work harder to process the chemicals, and some of it is a super stimulant that his body simply can't tolerate.

Recognising emotions can be a struggle for children who are on the spectrum. They can feel the energy of emotions but they don't know how to access, control nor communicate this - causing them stress. All or any of the above contribute to keeping your child on the 'stress hamster wheel'.

The combination of the internal and external stressors results in a stress response that simply doesn't switch off. If your child struggles at school because his senses feel bombarded or he is struggling to process the expectations of others about being social and popular, avoiding the school bully, being different or extremely clever, or simply being bored, it is this normal stress response that activates because the child feels threatened. He is terrified and stressed, and he may not have the vocabulary, the life experience or the power with which to express his feelings. He can't think straight, so he kicks out in angry and sometimes violent ways. Or perhaps he runs (fleeing), or he simply zones out (freezes). This was a recurring theme in some of our case studies.

Teaching children meditation is not trying to cure autism or other medical conditions, but it can help reduce the stress levels which may be exacerbating the behaviours of children on the spectrum.

In a working paper by the Centre of Child Development from Harvard University, there is evidence that toxic stress can have a negative impact on the developing brain of a child. If our children are stressed, it is going to be more challenging for them to learn - whether or not they have special needs.

## Balancing stress in the brain

Earlier I presented the benefits of meditation and how it can positively affect different parts of the brain. Here, we're going to explore three areas of the brain that relate to the stress response.

Alongside this, I'll introduce you to a mindful approach I call 'the amygdala hold' to help relax and bring your child out of his stress response.

The *amygdala* (as shown by the red dot in the picture below) lies in the centre of the skull, behind the brow, and deeper than the pineal gland. It is part of the brain's limbic system which influences functions such as emotion, behaviour, motivation, long term memory and sense of smell. It is also involved in the processing of emotional memories. The amygdala is almond-shaped, and has two sections, often referred to as *amygdalae*.

The *pre-frontal cortex* sits just behind our brow. This is our 'thinking brain', which allows us to think both rationally and creatively. This is known as 'executive functioning' which supports complex planning, decision making and social behaviour. Some children embrace one aspect more than the other: a creative thinker may produce amazing pieces of music or art, while failing to understand mathematical equations. Some children may have a logical approach to life so they might find it challenging to think creatively or use their imagination.

The *reptilian brain* lies at the base of the skull and with the help of the amygdala, engages the stress response. It is the oldest part of the brain, which is responsible for ensuring the survival of human species. In this day and age, we engage the thinking brain more frequently however the reptilian brain is still necessary for our survival as a member of the human species.

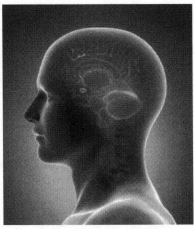

© iStock.com/janulla

A main function of the amygdala is to balance the brain's response to stimuli. If there is a threat, the amygdala activates the reptilian part of the brain to ensure we respond and support our survival (reaction). It also has other neural connections including the pre-frontal cortex which supports executive functioning (reflection and decision making).

## How can the amygdala and meditation help children with autism?

We can theorise that children on the autistic spectrum have an amygdala which is constantly active and firing up the reptilian brain. In other words these children are in a constant stress response.

*"The amygdala can orchestrate cognitive processes based on social stimuli, but it requires information about the context in which those stimuli occur — information conveyed by the prefrontal cortex and the hippocampus. In the absence of such contextual input, the amygdala may inappropriately interpret social stimuli, which may become ambiguous and overwhelming. The long-term effects of the concomitant anxiety and avoidance could add to social deficits."*

Dr Ralph Adolphs, Bren Professor of Psychology and Neuroscience, CIT

Meditation techniques can help children reduce their stress levels and reverse the effects of chronic stress; but in some cases this can be a struggle if they are in that heightened, stimulated stress state. Their survival instinct is so strong that it can be impossible to override it - but this is where the amygdala becomes a useful bedfellow.

If mindful awareness of the amygdala can create a 'bridge' between a child's reptilian brain and the pre-frontal cortex - we can move them out of their chronic stress state and strengthen the connection to executive functioning.

## Re-connecting the brain

So we want to encourage a child's reptilian brain to relax and let go. To do this, we encourage the connective energy of the amygdala to move forward and re-engage with the pre-frontal cortex involving the mindful, amygdala hold which is described below. With regular practice, stress will reduce and the reptilian brain will relax allowing the pre-frontal cortex to engage.

This isn't a complete solution, but we are taking a small step towards helping children out of their chronic stressed state. We would apply this before teaching a child what some view as traditional meditation methods (such as noticing the breath, paying attention to thoughts etc).

## Helping your child find his amygdala

During my research, I read a book called 'Tickle Your Amygdala' by Neil Slade.

The author interviews a variety of people ranging from movie stars to neurologists, all of whom have engaged in connecting their awareness to this part of the brain, either to influence or study it.

This extract describes how you can locate your amygdala:

> *"Place your thumbs against your ears and middle fingers on the outside corners of your eyes. About 25 mm inside your head from where your forefingers naturally come to rest on your temples is where your amygdalae reside."*

## A tactile approach

We can use visualisation and tactile methods to help engage awareness of the amygdala. Let's begin with the sense of touch. You'll experience positive results if you practise this regularly with kids in their normal state (e.g, not when they are in meltdown mode). Plus you'll teach them a life skill they can engage when you aren't there to support them.

## Amygdala hold no. 1- head in hands

*You can start by simply asking your child to hold the front of his head in the palms of his hands, with his elbows resting on a support. Guide him to sit like this for 10 to 30 seconds (count if necessary). Guide him to notice the sense of touch of his hands (warmth, coolness) and the weight of his head.*

*Repeat this mindful hold regularly so that your child can sit like this for up to a minute. It can help children if the parents/adults also engage in the amygdala hold; it helps them to copy your actions and it helps you feel calmer and less stressed. (Perhaps this is why we naturally sit with our head in our hands when we're stressed: we are trying to calm the amygdala!)*

## Amygdala hold no. 2 - holding their head

*Place one hand cupped around the forehead of your child while holding the back of the head with the other (where the base of the skull meets the neck). In this hold, you are connecting to both the 'thinking' and the 'reptilian' brain. Let your hands relax and imagine the word 'calm' written on the back of them. Take up to 10 deep, long 'belly breaths'; ask your child to do this too. Guide him to focus on his forehead: to be aware of the warmth or coolness of your hand, the shape of your hand, or how many of your fingers are touching. This can be done seated or lying down (e.g. before your child goes to sleep). If you are working with a group of children, you could guide them to do this for each other.*

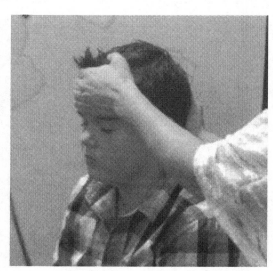

Credit: Breath Easy Kids

*"[the amygdala hold] makes me feel calm and relaxed like I'm floating in outer space."*

Jack, age 11
ADHD, GAD (Generalized Anxiety disorder)
and ODD (Oppositional Defiant Disorder)

## Amygdala hold no. 3 - self hold

*Here you are teaching your child to hold his own head just as you did in hold no. 2. You would guide him to do this and invite him to relax while thinking about his favourite toy, word, person, cartoon character or number (this will bring a positive emotion/feeling into his awareness).*

## Amygdala hold no. 4 - massaging the temples

*Stand behind your child and place your fingertips just behind his temples. Gently massage the temples in a circular motion; it is important that the motion is towards the forehead (pre-frontal cortex) as this directs him out of his stress response. If he chooses to massage his own temples you can blow gently on his forehead, so that he notices the sensation of touch on his brow. This will also help to keep his focus there.*

## Amygdala hold no. 5 - stroking the forehead

*Stand behind your child and simply trace your fingertips across his brow, alternating each hand. This becomes a rhythmical movement that can last up to 5 minutes. It can also be practised with your child lying down (head in your lap/pillow).*

*If your child doesn't enjoy your touch, you can teach him to do this. With practise you can help him to practise any of the above suggestions while inviting his breath to relax, and eventually his body. Remember he can practise on you too!*

## Why does this work?

Our sense of touch is governed by the somatic sensory system in our bodies. Along with smell, it is one of the most primitive ways we interpret life. Nerve receptors in our skin tell us when we are touching something, or when something is touching us.

These receptors send electrical signals through a complex wiring system in our bodies: special nerve cells called neurons play 'pass the parcel' with the signal until it reaches the spinal cord and then eventually the part of the brain (cerebellum) that manages this system.

When the brain receives the electrical message it interprets it and translates it before sending a different signal to a part of our body that can help, either by changing or maintaining something. For example, if we touch something too hot, the incoming signal from our hand relays this to our brain; and another signal is released from our brain to the muscles in our hand, telling it to let go of the hot stuff!

The sense of touch in the amygdala hold helps your child become aware of this part of his body. Emotions can be relayed through the sense of touch, which is why it is important for you to focus on your breath or think of the word 'calm' as you hold his head. If he is holding his own head in the amygdala hold, encourage him to think of the word 'calm'; alternatively he could look at a calming picture or something that makes him feel calm while holding his head.

## Using the imagination to engage the amygdala

Here are some ideas for you to try if your child has a good imagination.

Computer theme

While computers are processing information, we often see the icon of a spinning wheel. Ask your child to visualise this spinning wheel on the sides of his temples or in the centre of his head, and imagine that this spinning motion is moving forward in the direction of his forehead.

Action heroes or cartoon characters

Ask your child to imagine he is sitting with his favourite action hero or cartoon character. This character holds a fantastic device in his hand that has a light (like a torch), or whatever you feel is right for your child. The superhero is shining the light on his forehead which makes his forehead shine.

Hobbies

If your child has a hobby (such as trains), engage his imagination in using associated imagery to activate the amygdala. Perhaps he can imagine that he is sitting in the train and that the train is moving forward. Describe the rail tracks and the sound of the wheels moving forward. Ask him to imagine the smoke coming out of the front of the train and ask him to imagine that the smoke is just in front of his forehead (as if he were driving the train).

Each of these suggestions offer you a way to help your child connect his amygdala to the pre-frontal cortex using his imagination. If he practises these regularly during a less-stressed moment, he can then choose to apply it when he feels stressed, like a school classroom. Ensure his teachers are aware of this practice, so they can support the practice.

## Amygdala self help

If you have a child with autism or special needs, it's a good idea for you to practise the amygdala hold.

You may have been in a stressed state ever since you heard your child's diagnosis; or you may be anxious because you are still waiting to get one. Many parents tell me they've had to 'fight' for everything, which suggests to me that are in their stress response, feeling threatened.

It's important to address your needs and those of any other family members and people who come into regular contact with your child. I've already talked about how children reflect our own emotional state, so you can see why it's important for us to balance our own energy.

If you can practise this visualisation technique throughout your day, it can help keep your stress levels balanced.

Here is an extract from 'Tickle Your Amygdala' by Neil Slade:

*"Visualise a feather softly tickling the anterior (forward) part of the amygdala, first on one side, then the other. If you prefer, use a pair of feathers and do both sides at the same time. That's all there is to it. Just remember, gentleness (you're using a feather, not a cattle prod!) and directing energy forward, into the frontal lobes, are the keys to success."*

By practising this, you are helping both you *and* your child.

*"I love the amygdala hold. I use it every time I put Evan to bed, and sometimes just when he is sitting beside me. My husband also uses one hand on the back of Evan's neck, as he finds it difficult to use both hands. Evan has tried a few times to do this on his own, but it will take more practise. The hold settles him really quickly, sometimes within a minute. I just hold his head when I know he has gone to sleep - his breathing is steady and he looks so peaceful. It feels like, if I take my hands away, he will lose what is probably the least anxious time of his day."*

Donna, Mum (case study)

## Mirror neurons

Mirror neurons were discovered in the 1990's and are useful for us to consider when teaching children with additional support needs.

If your child performs an activity, certain cells in his brain light up to show they are active. This has been confirmed through science with MRI scans (magnetic resonance imaging).

If you perform an activity and your child watches you, both your brain cells and the same ones in your child's brain become active; this is what we call 'mirror neurons' (neurons are the nerve cells in the brain).

Science and psychology both argue that these neurons are essential for explaining how we come to understand another's behaviour and their intentions. Also they help us understand why imitating someone can help us learn new skills. If there is a lack of mirror neurons, then we lack empathy. A theory has been proposed that autism is linked to this lack of mirror neurons.

My interest in mirror neurons relates to working with children who have a physical disability that prevents them from taking part in some mindful activities. If we perform yoga moves, doe their mirror neurons fire and the body respond as if they were practising yoga? If we do this with children, will it help them feel calmer and more peaceful as if they were meditating?

I have no concrete answer to give you, but I wanted to plant the seed. What I can offer is an interesting response by a child with cerebral palsy who couldn't physically complete a mandala, but watched as other people coloured them.

> *"My 4 year old nephew has severe cerebral palsy. He can't stand unaided, only speaks a few words and doesn't have much control of his hands/arms. He is very active with leg kicking and wriggling most of the time, but he loves watching people colour pictures for him. Watching him choose the colours and which bit he wants you to colour by nodding, he becomes totally still and focused. He'll watch you colour several pictures for him for a long time. It is absolutely wonderful to see."*

Julie Woolrich-Moon, Connected Kids Tutor

## Centering thought for your personal meditation practice

If a non-stressed brain absorbs information more easily and helps neurological development, could teaching your child meditation help him to relax, de-stress and improve his learning?

# 13. YOGA, MUDRAS AND MASSAGE

*"Yoga is not about self-improvement, it's about self-acceptance."*

*Gurmukh Kaur Khalsa, Yoga Teacher and Author*

Yoga is a form of moving meditation which, like sitting meditation, has been practised for thousands of years. Some view it as a physical way to keep fit or improve flexibility while others also recognise the potential to explore the spiritual nature of the body through mindful movement.

Dating back to 900 BC, it is part of the Ayurvedic system of health which has its roots in Indian culture. While yoga has many variations and schools, its ultimate purpose is to help bring mind, body, emotions and spirit into balance with each other. It is now internationally recognised as an excellent way to introduce meditation to children and teens.

Many people who practise meditation, yoga and healing believe that the physical body can hold accumulated emotions and mental energy; thus the physical state of the body reflects how we are feeling and thinking.

Our emotional and mental state can be expressed through the physical body. Think of what happens when we are embarrassed: our perception of a situation feeds our thoughts, which link to our feelings of embarrassment, and our body may respond with blushing - a physical widening of the blood vessels in the face where blood rushes to the skin. This is part of the sympathetic nervous system which links to the stress response. So the physical response of blushing is stimulated by our emotional and mental state.

Imagine your child feels angry and clenches his hands and jaw. If this emotion and the associated thoughts are not expressed and processed, these muscles are tightened repeatedly, resulting in that part of the body becoming less flexible and even painful in the long

146

term. This response can be become second nature, and even pass unnoticed until pain appears.

## Emotionally balanced through flexibility

As a baby, your child may have wonderful flexibility; usually this relates to his state of emotional freedom. But if challenging emotions and mental states aren't processed in a healthy way, as he gets older this may manifest as physical inflexibility. If we teach children yoga, we can help their physical, emotional and mental states to remain flexible and strong.

Those on the Connected Kids programme taught me how teaching children yoga helps them come into balance. In the case studies, yoga was suggested where children with attention issues could not sit still to meditate. The practice settled their energy, helping them to meditate more peacefully.

*Credit : Kay Locke and Space4Autism*
(Teens on the autistic spectrum practising a form of
the warrior yoga pose; sometimes called 'surfer')

When children practise yoga they are not only exercising their body, but they are helping it to process emotions and thoughts. The physical movement helps clear and release blockages of energy. A Connected Kids tutor described how silent tears ran down children's cheeks during a relaxation and meditation session (following yoga). This is the body releasing the stressful emotions that have been building up. You may think that a child crying after meditation isn't a positive outcome, yet we release a large amount of a stress hormone, cortisol, through our tears; the body's natural response as it comes back into balance.

Parents and educators of autistic children are aware of rigid behaviours, which may be linked with inflexibility in the body. Introducing mindful activities may bring about a physical sense of relaxation, and more flexibility within routines as a result of a more relaxed emotional and mental state.

One of our tutors, Kay Locke, was diagnosed with Asperger syndrome (AS) and has two daughters with the same condition. Kay is a yoga teacher for children with special needs. She explains some of the benefits of teaching children yoga:

> *"As an individual with AS I was initially motivated to practise yoga entirely for the perceived physical benefit; to maintain and promote physical health. However, studying yoga teacher training informed me of the entire spectrum, aims and philosophy of yoga, including meditation. Relaxation and meditation are the two key factors that have proved valuable in promoting coping strategies as an individual with AS."*

## How yoga can help kids with special needs

For some children with additional support needs, there can be issues with balance, movement and sensory processing which has built up a state of chronic stress. Yoga and meditation helps to redress this.

## The Vestibular system

Within the body the ears form part of the vestibular system. Along with our visual system and the proprioceptors in our muscles and joints, it helps us to determine spatial awareness; where our body sits in space in relation to other objects and where the limbs are in relation to our body. Alongside the senses, this information is relayed through our nervous system to the brain.

When our vestibular system isn't functioning or working as effectively, we can feel disorientated and dizzy. A child on the spectrum may struggle to know where his physical body begins and ends. The information isn't being processed to his brain so it makes 'being in his body' an uncertain and stressful experience.

## The Psoas muscle

Sometimes this is referred to as "the soul muscle" as it holds everything together. Deep within the core of the body, it is the only muscle that attaches our core to our legs. Author and expert Liz Koch explains

> *"Intimately involved in the fight or flight response, the psoas can curl you into a protective fetal ball or flex you to prepare the powerful back and leg muscles to spring into action. Because the psoas is so intimately involved in such basic physical and emotional reactions, a chronically tightened psoas continually signals your body that you're in danger, eventually exhausting the adrenal glands and depleting the immune system. As you learn to approach the world without this chronic tension, psoas awareness can open the door to a more sensitive attunement to your body's inner signals about safety and danger, and to a greater sense of inner peace."*

Liz Koch, Author of 'The Psoas Book'

Teaching children yoga with the intention of relaxing the psoas muscle allows it to 'speak'. This can help children connect to their bodies with more mindfulness and release the stress that has accumulated over time (e.g. children become more present and feel more grounded). Because of the body, mind and emotions connection, the balancing of the physical body has a positive and balancing effect on the emotional and mental states of your children.

A simple way to start to relax the psoas muscle is to have a child lie on his back, knees bent and feet flat on the floor while you guide them in meditation.

As your child becomes less stressed, he can then use his meditation practise (mindful of breath and body) to develop a coping system for the challenges of life.

Consider how some children with autism walk on their toes or rock or feel calmer when bouncing on a trampoline. Perhaps they are naturally trying to engage the core and bring inner balance and peace?

## Yoga meditation postures

Yoga teachers undergo thorough training, and I recommend that you take your children to a yoga class for kids in order to gain the most benefits. I particularly recommend those teachers who are trained in teaching yoga to children with special needs. However, I appreciate that you may be curious as to what yoga is and how it may help your child.

Here are some simple yoga moves that you can do with children. I have given short descriptions, and you'll find links to online videos on YouTube.

**Child's pose** (helps to relax mind and body)

Ask your child to kneel and sit on her heels. Then ask her to lean forward and touch her head on the floor. If her hips start to lift off her heels, put a cushion or two under her forehead for support. Her arms can stretch out in front or by her sides with the palms of her hands facing up (as shown).

As she practises, guide her to breathe a colour in and out of her chakras or different parts of her spine; you could also touch the different parts of her spine, asking her to focus and breathe into that spot as you work down the spine.

This position stretches out the back and it also helps to release any energy tension in the chakras all down the spine.

(In addition to the posture, the pressure of touch on the forehead has a similar effect to the amygdala hold, as explained in Chapter 12 - 'Calming *the nervous system*').

**Mountain pose** (helps with grounding and stability)

Start by asking your child to stand with her hands hanging at her sides and her chin slightly tucked in. Ask her to imagine there is a golden thread attached to the top of her head, pulling it gently up towards the sky, stretching her neck.

Suggest that her knees feel soft; ask her to pull in her tummy to help her core feel a bit stronger. Invite her to stretch out her toes so her feet are as flat as possible on the ground - as if her feet were like suckers, pulling up the energy of the Earth. Suggest that she can think about a mountain and silently say: "Breathing in, my body is strong like a mountain; breathing out, my body is strong".

*Here are some more yoga poses that you could research:*

**Lion pose** - releases tension in face and chest, helps with respiratory issues

**Tree pose** - good for grounding, improves stability and self esteem

**Crocodile pose** - helps grounding and balancing (links in to the effects of the amygdala hold)

**Cobra/sphinx** - opens up heart centre chakra, relieves stress

**Fish pose** - opens the heart chakra and balances energy in the solar plexus (releasing the need to control, developing trust).

**Crab pose** - opens the heart chakra and balances energy in the solar plexus (releasing the need to control, developing trust).

*Top Row (left to right) - Lion, Tree, Crocodile and Sphinx.*
*Bottom Row (left to right) - Cobra, Fish and Crab*

Each yoga pose gives your child a moving form of meditation, or a way to hold his body in meditation and silence while focusing on his breath.

## Yoga Breathing

In yoga, the breath is equally as important as the posture or movement. The alternate nostril breathing is a way to help calm the body. You can follow the instructions below (for your own self practice in addition to teaching children).

## Alternative Nostril Breath

*Invite your child to sit comfortably*

*He rests his left hand on his left knee*

*With his right hand, he touches his forehead with the tip of his index and middle finger (between the eyebrows)*

*His thumb connects to his right nostril and his ring finger connects to the left.*

*Invite him to close of the right nostril with his thumb and breathe out through the left nostril. Then breathe in through the left nostril.*

*Invite him to close of his left nostril with his ring finger and breathe out through right nostril. Then breathe in through his right nostril.*

*Repeat steps 5 and 6 for up to 7 breaths.*

## Mudras - 'hand yoga'

There are many nerve endings in our fingers which link into our nervous system. When you massage and press points on the feet or hands, this affects the nerve endings that congregate in these areas, sending calming or stimulating signals to the brain and the nervous system, all of which connect to major systems and organs of the body. Also consider that massaging energy points in the hands will also help stimulate or calm the flow of energy in the body's major chakras.

If the hands are stiff or inflexible, this can suggest inflexibility in emotions or thoughts and a restriction in the flow of energy in the body.

A mudra is a posture held with by the fingers during meditation; it connects energy points and nerve endings in the fingers. By holding a mudra for a specific length of time, the body brings itself back into balance with a calmer state of consciousness. As the flexibility in the hands increases, the energy flows and emotions and thoughts can be released and come into balance.

Mudras are often used to help with insomnia, stomach complaints, constipation, and anxiety; there is even a mudra that can help reduce the effects of tension or asthma.

In 'Calm Kids', I describe a couple of mudras which will help your child to ground his energy, aiding focus and concentration. They can also help settle your energy if you've had a challenging day.

While mudras are a great tool teaching meditation, they are an easy way for children to practice a calming technique while walking, sitting in the car or bus, or before any stressful situation. In this way, children can learn to self-regulate their emotions by simply connecting their fingers in specific patterns.

If mudras are combined with meditation practice or a mindful activity, it can elevate the response. Combining mudras with meditations on colour, the breath or with words and affirmations can enhance the effects.

If a child can't hold a yoga posture, he can hold a hand mudra as a useful alternative to help bring in more flexibility and balance for his energy.

## Copy Cat

When you are asking your child to practise these hand positions, it's a good idea for you to do it with him so that he can imitate. As you ask him to focus on his breath holding the mudra, you can invite him to use imagery, words or colour to keep his attention.

If it's difficult for your child to concentrate, place his favourite toy in front of him and ask him to focus on this as he holds the mudra - looking at the shape and the colours, and thinking about how much he likes to play with it. Consider inviting younger children to make a shadow with the shape, which will hold their interest as they make the hand posture.

If your child has any difficulty in holding a mudra, don't force it or you could gently hold his hands in the mudra position.

Younger children may be uninterested or confused by the sounds of the names of these mudras, so I have thought of alternative 'playful' names (feel free to create your own!)

**Hakini Mudra** (or 'windy mudra', as it connects with the breath)

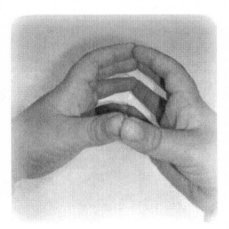

This mudra is said to balance the left and right hemispheres of the brain, and is taught as a management mind training technique. It can have a positive effect on the lungs, so it could be helpful for children with asthma or breathing problems. By practising this mudra, we are giving children with special needs or high stress levels the opportunity to come out of the stress response by deepening their breath.

The Hakini mudra involves the fingertips of each hand touching, as shown. Here are a few ways in which you can guide your child to use it:

Option 1 - ask him to think of a triangle or pyramid as he holds the mudra for a few breaths.

Option 2 - do the same as above but to help him focus on the breath, ask him to place his hands to his mouth; as he breathes out, he will feel his breath flow through the space between his hands. An alternative is to ask him to move his hands so that it is just his fingertips at his mouth; again, he will notice the touch of his breath on his fingers. (Do this for between one and 10 breaths, depending on the attention span of your child. Perhaps start with a couple of breaths and build up to 10.

Option 3 - holding the Hakini mudra, ask him to place his hands so that his thumbs are touching his forehead. On the out breath, release the thumbs and let him stroke the forehead with his fingertips. Do this between one and five times. Ask him to focus on the touch of his fingers on this part of his head.

Option 4 - ask him to hold the mudra and focus on imagery that involves the breath: blowing up a balloon, blowing out a candle, the wind blowing a kite or the wind blowing the sails in a boat; using descriptive imagery like this can help support his concentration.

## Guided Meditation for Hakini Mudra

*With the palms touching, ask your child to imagine blowing up a balloon*

*Each time he breathes out, the finger tips keep touching but the space in his hands gets bigger.*

*After several breaths he's holding the hakini mudra.*

*On one final breath his hands separate and he can shake his hands to release any stress.*

**Pran Mudra** (or 'muddy mudra', as it connects to the Earth)

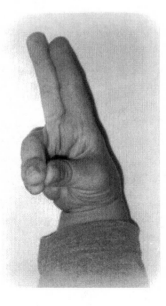

This is helpful for ADHD, as it balances the root chakra.

The Pran mudra also balances the adrenals and the nervous system; it balances the left and right hemispheres of the brain and can calm the limbic system, which affects our hormonal and emotional responses. It can be helpful in a meditation or used regularly throughout the day.

Combining this mudra with a guided meditation where the imagery is grounding (e.g. a tree) can be an effective way to help children feel more centred and calm.

*Invite your child to let the tips of the thumb, the ring finger and pinkie connect on each hand.*

*Guide him to stretch out the remaining two fingers.*

*Hold for 1 to 5 minutes.*

**Apan Mudra** (or 'deer mudra' because it looks like a deer's head)

This mudra is good for detoxing the body and helping with constipation, which I have noticed is an issue for many autistic children; it is said to balance the liver and gall bladder.

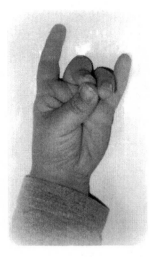

*Guide your child to touch the tip of the middle and ring finger to the tip of the thumb.*

*The index and pinkie stretch out.*

*While holding this mudra, guide him to imagine a seed growing in the ground.*

*Invite him to imagine what it needs to grow (earth, water, sunshine).*

*The seed starts to let go of its original casing as it expands into a flower, a tree or a plant.*

*The plant puts down roots; absorbing what it needs, and letting go of what it doesn't need in order to grow.*

*Hold for 1 to 5 minutes.*

**Mukula Mudra** (or 'light beam mudra')

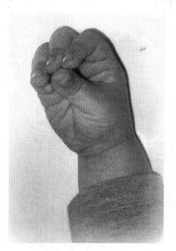

The Mukula mudra helps with easing pain or stress in the body (including asthma). It is said to create a laser-like quality of energy at the finger tips that takes out the energy toxins and brings in the energy 'power'.

*Guide your child to touch the tip of his thumb with the tips of all the other fingers.*

*He then places it on the part of the body that is causing discomfort.*

*Invite him to think or silently repeat the words "power in" (in breath) and "pain out" out breath as he holds the mudra.*

*Hold for 1 to 5 minutes.*

He can choose the words he wants, but the affirmation helps to enhance the effect. I taught this to a client who had asthma and couldn't stop coughing: she held this mudra, and within minutes the coughing had stopped.

## Varuna Mudra (or 'water' mudra)

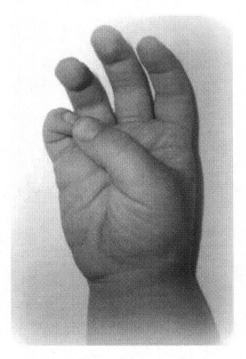

This can help with constipation and indigestion problems. As our bodies are 60 to 70% water (higher in children) so hydration is important. This mudra is said to help balance the water in our bodies so it may be useful in helping children who find it difficult to drink water regularly. It can help clear excess mucous in the body.

*Invite your child to bend the small finger on his right hand so that its tip touches the base of the thumb.*

*Guide him to use the left hand around the right for support, and the left thumb to hold the fingers in place.*

*Hold for 1 to 5 minutes.*

*Repeat as required.*

Perhaps while holding this mudra, take them on a guided meditation involving water - swimming in the sea, standing under a waterfall or the rain.

Credit: Yoga Poses and Mudras - Piper & Marshall from Little Yogis School

## Mindful Mudras

If children have a short attention span, asking them to sit and hold a mudra may be a bit challenging! One way around this is to combine the mudra with the breath and perhaps encourage some movement between the fingers.

Here is a practice which they can do with both hands:

*Guide your child to start with the tip of the thumb and his first finger touching on each hand*

*On the in-breath the thumb and first fingertip touch*

*On the out-breath the fingers open*

*Repeat several times.*

*Then he moves the tip of his thumb to the tip of the middle finger, touching the tip of the thumb with as he breathes in*

*He opens his fingers as he breathes out*

*Repeat several times*

*Guide him to move on to the ring finger and then the little finger, repeating the breaths as above*

*Then guide him to work his way back from the little finger to the forefinger, repeating the breath sequence.*

Once you have done this several times, help your child to think of their favourite word, colour, or image or perhaps a number that he can now associate with this movement.

## Mindful massage

Massage is a tactile way to help the body come into balance. Because of the position of nerve receptors in the upper body, it can be very relaxing for your child to have a face or head massage.

One of my colleagues, Helen Harris, has trained in this technique with Indian Champissage International, and she has suggested this short practice which you may wish to try at home. It is advisable to try the massage on yourself first before attempting to practise it on your child, just to ensure that you can do it in a relaxed way. This avoids your tension or anxiety transferring to him through your hands.

Treat the act of massage as a moving meditation, paying attention to the sense of touch, your breath and the position of your body. Ask your child to give feedback on the pressure and pace. You could also ask him to practise on you, which then becomes a moving meditation for him and you are then sharing the mindful experience.

## Face massage

*"Natural Facelift Massage involves the use of specific techniques to tone the face and reduce the signs of stress and ageing. However there are some who have found that its effects go deeper, in particular its ability to calm and reduce anxiety.*

*There are no creams or lotions involved. Contact between the practitioner and the receiver is direct and firm. Some of techniques would be worth trying with a child with autism, given the increasing number of reports in the literature about the benefits of firm massage for children with this condition. The treatment also involves the use of acupressure points requiring firm pressure.*

*The technique used to free muscular tension in the face involves the use of four or five finger pads of both hands moving in an outward circular motion, beginning in the middle of the forehead and working out to the temples, then from either side of the nose out towards the ears and finally from either side of the mouth out across the jaw.*

*A second technique connects with the forehead. The finger pads of one hand are placed just below the hairline and they gently tauten the skin.*

*The fleshy pad at base of thumb, of the other hand, firmly sweeps across the forehead from level with the outer eyebrow to the middle of the forehead.*

*Then the hands are swapped and the sweep is in the opposite direction. The moves are repeated on the other side of the forehead.*

*Potentially useful acupressure points include those shown in the illustration. Firm finger pressure is used on each point for up to a minute."*

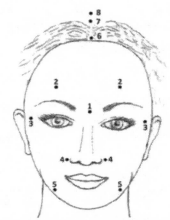

*Credit : London Centre of Indian Champissage*

## Centering thought for your personal meditation practice

Which of the mudras, massage or yoga postures would most benefit your child?

# 14. DEVELOPING EMOTIONAL AWARENESS

*"Everything that irritates us about others, can lead us to an understanding of ourselves."*

*Carl Jung, Psychiatrist*

Some assume that meditation offers a constant feeling of peace. In one sense this is true but only once we accept our human emotions. Meditation helps a child to acknowledge and process emotions. Eventually he learns to accept these feelings which helps him to develop compassion for himself and others.

There's a powerful connection between the emotions, thoughts and the body. The first step is recognising the presence of emotions. When we feel angry, can we identify how our bodies react, what we are thinking and how we are feeling? Until we notice this, we can't change or accept it. The same is true for toddlers to teens.

When we don't understand our emotions or don't want to acknowledge them, this causes a disturbance in our energy; it causes us stress. If we witness the emotions with mindful acceptance, only then can we have peace with them. This self-acceptance helps us develop emotional intelligence. This is a valuable skill that mediation can teach our children.

Daniel Goleman, author of 'Emotional Intelligence', explains:

> *"In 1995, I outlined the preliminary evidence suggesting that SEL [social and emotional learning] was the active ingredient in programs that enhance children's learning while preventing problems such as violence. Now the case can be made scientifically: helping children improve their self-awareness and confidence, managing their disturbing emotions and impulses, and increasing their empathy pays off not just in improved behavior but in measurable academic achievement."*

Often we push these emotions down inside by ignoring and pretending they aren't there because we don't know what to do with them (and they feel quite uncomfortable). As time passes we know these emotions exist but find it more difficult to ignore them. We start to mask them with addictions like alcohol, work, food, shopping, exercise or drugs. This works for a period until there is an emotional 'explosion' that can present itself physically or mentally.

If we teach children how to meditate, we are giving them the space and freedom to feel and express their emotions in a mindful and healing way, without the need to go through this emotional stressful journey.

Just because I teach and practise meditation doesn't mean I don't feel irritated, angry or upset sometimes. I honour those feelings by feeling them in my body, breathing into them and accepting them. Usually I can do this at the time the emotion rises. Sometimes I take time out to reflect and 'sit' with the feeling.

Bach Flower therapist, Linsey Denham, talks about secondary emotions. First of all we have a feeling of anger. Then we have a feeling of guilt or worry about being angry. All emotions are real and valid, so it is healing to acknowledge all of them - mindfully.

The following poem by the 13th century poet, Rumi, helped me cope with strong emotions;

*The Guest House*

*This being human is a guest house.*
*Every morning a new arrival.*
*A joy, a depression, a meanness,*
*some momentary awareness comes*
*as an unexpected visitor.*

*Welcome and entertain them all!*
*Even if they are a crowd of sorrows,*
*who violently sweep your house*
*empty of its furniture,*
*still, treat each guest honorably.*
*He may be clearing you out*
*for some new delight.*

*The dark thought, the shame, the malice.*
*meet them at the door laughing and invite them in.*

*Be grateful for whatever comes.*
*because each has been sent*
*as a guide from beyond.*

(Translation by Coleman Barks)

A psychotherapist told me that most of his clients were dealing with 'inner child' emotions that were related to incidents in childhood. He felt that, had they been able to feel and express these at the time, they could have avoided therapy in adult life.

## Releasing our expectations

When you teach children meditation you may think that is the most important part. You start to imagine that your child will be happier, quieter and more peaceful. If that doesn't happen, you can feel you've done something wrong or that meditation doesn't work.

The following examples show how children processed difficult and challenging emotions after their meditation.

A teacher in Thailand wrote to me asking for advice. She had taught her class meditation, but one of the children had been upset and in tears. When I asked more questions, it transpired that the girl's mother was in prison in Burma. I imagine that this child was feeling the stress, anxiety and fear that any of us would feel in this situation, but until the meditation she had not had the opportunity to truly feel and express it. This was a healing step for this child as tears contain a high percentage of the stress hormone, cortisol.

A head teacher who teaches children yoga and meditation told me how following the practice, one of the boys had an angry fight with another child. The head teacher could not understand why. I suggested that the meditation had released those feelings; if she gave him the chance to express it after the meditation through writing, drawing or speaking, this would have helped him process this more peacefully.

We may think that the meditation practice is the most valuable part of the experience for children but the processing continues beyond this; expressing and sharing the experience is as valuable as the meditation itself.

## Sharing mindfully

I learned how to listen and share mindfully and compassionately when I attended an educators' retreat with Thich Nhat Hanh. The audience would split into smaller groups with the purpose of inviting each person to express their feelings and thoughts about the retreat.

We practised mindful listening and talking as we shared our thoughts and feelings. With repeated practise, even the quieter group members began to contribute to the session; they found the space to open up.

As we listened to each other, we were also mindful of our own thoughts and emotions. I found myself feeling irritated with some people who appeared to pay little attention to the person speaking; but with mindful awareness it helped me recognise, accept and release my expectations of how they should behave.

I found it amazing just to listen with my breath and with the awareness of my body; most of all, I focused on my heart as I listened. We didn't try to offer each other solutions; we simply listened with an open heart.

## Compassionate listening and talking

When we listen to what another human being has to say with an open heart, they can feel it with their heart on a level beyond thought and mind, and it can help them to say what they truly feel. When sharing, if we are mindful in our words and speak from our own heart, it touches others in a healing way. This experience brought home the powerful effects of sharing and listening from the heart. The opposite is to listen with the 'mind'. As they speak, we are already working out what we want to say or the solutions we can give. This leaves our child feeling 'unheard'.

If you are teaching children to meditate, either one-to-one or in a group, there are some excellent ways to help them to share their experiences after the meditation in a heartfelt way.

## The 'Namaste bow'

If you intend to teach a child or group of children over several sessions, the following is a helpful way to introduce mindful listening and talking.

Often when we ask a child or teen a question, it is likely that while we are waiting to hear their words we have anticipated how they will respond. I believe children feel this pressure and if we learn to practise mindful listening (especially after a meditation practice) we give that child the space to share.

I would suggest listening compassionately with an open heart, without interrupting. Even nodding your head repeatedly and 'mms' or 'ahs' can be quite distracting. If you wish, you can ask a question, but give your child the time and space to answer. Practise your mindful breathing during these moments if you find it difficult to be quiet and place one hand on your chest to remind yourself of your heart chakra.

On the retreat, I found a powerful way to encourage others to speak - I call it the 'Namaste bow'. Since then I have brought it into all my 'Connected Kids' courses and meditation groups.

This is what 'Namaste' means:

> *"I honour the place in you where Spirit lives*
> *I honour the place in you which is*
> *of Love, of Truth, of Light, of Peace;*
> *When you are in that place in you,*
> *and I am in that place in me,*
> *then we are One."*

Simply ask children to place their hands together in the Namaste position - the prayer position - at their chest. This is not intended to be a religious gesture, but if anyone is uncomfortable with it, you can ask them to bring their hands together at their heart centre, one palm resting gently on top of the other. In doing this, they are acknowledging their heart centre and bringing it into their awareness.

When a child is ready to speak, he nods or bows to the others in the group; this sends the signal to others that someone is about to speak.

The others bow back to the speaker in the same way, to acknowledge that they have heard this request and are ready to listen mindfully with an open heart.

Depending on the age group, you could explain this to children by saying that, when they nod, it's as if they are offering the other person a gift from their heart - perhaps a flower, a smile, or a rainbow. It is the intention behind the 'bow' that is important as it will be reflected back to them.

Once the child bows in, no one interrupts; all must wait until the child has finished speaking. If someone does interrupt, then they aren't listening mindfully. Each child is invited to speak but it is their choice. If you sit in silence, check in with your own breath and wait to see if more children are ready to share. When they have finished speaking, the child bows once again (to signal they have finished) and the group bows back.

This can be a very moving experience, and you might like to do this with every meditation that you teach. I encourage you to bow in to share so that your children can hear you speak truthfully from your heart - not as the 'adult', but as *you*. Children will feel and recognise your sincerity, and you will be teaching them a wonderful lesson of speaking your truth.

## Talking feather or stick

If you feel that the Namaste bow may not be suitable, you could bring in a 'talking feather' or a 'talking stick'. The guidelines are the same as for the Namaste bow: whoever holds the feather or stick has a turn to speak. The others pay full, mindful attention to that person's words and to how they feel while they are listening to them.

## Expressing feelings through art

You could invite your child to express his experience of the meditation, or simply reflect how he is feeling at that particular moment, on paper. This way, he can share his feelings through shape and colour; you may also be able to see if what he draws changes over time, as he processes his feelings.

Encourage your child to pay attention to the colours he likes and how he feels as he draws, noticing his breath and how his body feels. Afterwards, ask him if it makes him feel happy or sad. There is no judgment about the drawing, and he can choose whether or not to keep it.

When we draw, we are accessing the right side of our brain, and connecting with the imagination. If your child isn't able to do this, you could give him a picture to colour instead.

Remember that a mandala can also be used to process emotions arising from after meditation.

© Connected Kids Ltd

One of my friends, who was suffering from cancer, found that her five-year-old daughter was having anxiety attacks. We were concerned about her, so we did a short meditation which I call the 'thank you meditation' (see Chapter 6 - 'Connecting to heart centre intelligence').

174

After the meditation she decided to draw a picture. She drew me with big wings (I think I look like an angel!) The colours she chose were turquoise - linked to the throat chakra - and purple, which represents the big picture of the brow and crown chakras; big 'stuff' was going on in her life and her throat was trying to express these feelings.

## Writing

Another way to express emotions is by writing. If the child is able to write, he could write down any words or sentences that express his meditation. He may like to use coloured pens, choosing colours to express his feelings. You could ask him to write one word and then turn it into a picture using the coloured pens.

Your child might like to create a wall of meditation pictures, or a meditation diary where he can write and draw. This allows him to create a regular practice and a way of letting go of what he feels.

## Movement

In one of our 'Connected Kids' sessions we talked about movement - inviting children to move or do yoga postures can help them express their feelings. Movement helps with grounding and it balances the sacral chakra, helping children to release any emotional baggage that they can't find the words to express.

## Grounding strong emotions

It helps to ground and release any strong emotions that come up. We can gently guide them through this. Touching the earth is a practice that allows children of all ages to acknowledge their feelings but let it pass through them like a wave.

## Touching the Earth

Any kind of strong emotion (anger, upset or feeling agitated) can benefit from this mindful activity.

*Invite your child to lie on the ground with the front of his body touching the ground and arms and legs stretched out like 'superman'.*

*Guide him to stretch his body, then relax (this can be repeated if you feel it is necessary).*

*Invite him to notice all the different points of touch between his body and the ground; (forehead, arms, chest, tummy, hips, legs etc.).*

*Guide him to notice his breath and what he is feeling.*

*With each breath he releases this feeling into the ground through every point of his body.*

*Guide him to imagine that the earth absorbs all these difficult or heavy feelings. He doesn't have to carry them anymore. He can let them go with each breath.*

If we practise mindfulness of our emotions and teach our children and young people to honour and process them, the after effects of the emotions will not linger, influencing future life decisions.

## Connecting our emotions to the body

The body is a great teacher and gives us many clues about what we need to come into balance. For example, you receive a signal that your body needs to visit the bathroom. When you do it brings your body (chemically) back into balance. It is how we potty train our children so that they learn to stop using nappies.

Our body also gives us signals when we are stressed or becoming upset. If we become aware of this connection between the body and the feeling, then we can make a conscious choice. This is how we can support children when they experience stressful emotions. Before it even reaches an intense stage, children can learn that different body signals indicate feeling unhappy, angry, upset or any other difficult emotion they can name.

When they become aware of this, they can use the breath or the 'hook up' (see below) to become more relaxed and reverse the stress response.

It teaches children self-regulation. They become responsible for their feelings and how to manage them, rather than going straight to a place of fear, anger or emotional overload.

## The Hook-up

From the research based on Donna Eden's work (an energy expert) this is a very simply technique that can help anyone (child/adult/teen) feel calmer at the onset of stress. For over 30 years she has been teaching energy techniques to help people of all ages to naturally bring their health back to balance.

> *Place the tip of one middle finger on the brow and the tip of the other middle finger on the belly button.*
>
> *Pull in and up and hold this for about 20 seconds - while focussing on breathing deeply.*
>
> *Let go of the hold.*

This taps into energy points in the body and if practised regularly, it can be an effective mindful tool to take the heat out of oncoming stress.

It is important to practise this hold with children when they aren't feeling upset so they know what to do. Then make a promise that they (and you) hold that position if they start to feel anxious or upset.

## Centering thought for your personal meditation practice

How do you check in with your feelings and express strong emotions?

# 15. MINDFUL ACTIVITIES FOR AUTISM

In the first book, Calm Kids, I gave examples of how symptoms of ADHD can connect to imbalances in the chakra energy system. In this book I offer a theory that connects imbalances in the chakras with autism. If you have experienced autism, you will know that each person is a unique. Reading through the list will help you to identify a link between your child and certain chakras but not all issues will apply to your child. If you are able to identify energy centres that appear to be out of balance in your child, refer to the suggestions below to help him reduce the stress he feels when a part of his energy system is out of balance.

More detailed information about these suggestions can be found throughout Part 2 - Your meditation toolkit. There are some useful ideas in the Calm Kids book too. Remember to trust your intuition when choosing a mindful activity for your child with autism - the following is only a guide!

## Chakra: Root

**Relates to:** Connection to the world through physical security and energy

**Root Issues in Autism:**

- Feeling ungrounded, the child feels as if they are from another planet; difficulties with physical senses and adapting to the environment - air, pollution, food, chemicals, light, sound and sense of touch.

- Feeling threatened - in the fight, flight or freeze response (the root and solar plexus chakras link to the adrenal glands which activate our stress response).

- Lack of cross connection between left and right brain hemispheres can create a sensation of feeling out of balance and 'off-centre'.

- Constant grazing of food; eating is a way to ground energy (taking in physical food and attempting to 'weigh down' energy through the body).

- Hoarding; similar to eating where children feel the need to 'collect' and surround themselves with physical items. This relates to the need to manifest a physical presence on earth and feel safe.

- Fixation; a child can fixate on something to help establish a frame of reference when the rest of the world feels 'fluid'. The 'fluidity' of energy comes from interference from emotions and thoughts of others, chemical and bodily changes within themselves and electromagnetic frequencies and an imbalance in the psoas muscle.

Social Skills: Difficulty in following conversations or group interactions.
*Observations* - Stress affects ability to concentrate.
*Balancing Mindful Activities* - Placing hand on chest and focussing on the sense of touch of chest and hand while others are speaking.

Movement/Body: Walking on toes
*Observations* - Ungrounded
*Balancing Mindful Activities* - Engaging core through yoga moves **or** foot massage (both administered and self massage).
*Additional Info* - Engaging core - Chapter 13

Movement/Body: Unusual gait and walking style.
*Observations* - Ungrounded as if gravity isn't functioning.
*Balancing Mindful Activities* - Golden spacesuit meditation **or**

foot massage.
*Additional Info* - Engaging core - Chapter 13

Movement/Body: Odd posture (rigid/floppy).
*Observations* - Rigid - fight/flight/freeze response. Floppy - poor core.
*Balancing Mindful Activities* - Yoga postures to improve core **or** grounding crystal or stone in each pocket to help balance energy.
*Additional Info* - Yoga Postures - Chapter 13, Grounding crystal - Calm Kids book

Social Skills: Lack of personal space.
*Also links to* - aura
*Observations* - Personal energy field malfunction.
*Balancing Mindful Activities* - Using guided imagery to teach about being an arm's length distance to people **or** self bubble image - use in guided meditation to help create safe distance. Using colour to strengthen their personal space.
*Additional Info* - Self bubble image - Chapter 8.

Behaviours: Collections of items.
*Also links to* - brow chakra
*Observations* - Ungrounded
*Balancing Mindful Activities* - Guided meditation to imagine filling pockets with their collections; feeling heavier and safe.

Behaviours: Unusual attachment to objects.
*Also links to* - brow chakra, aura
*Observations* - Items are like a comfort blanket.
*Balancing Mindful Activities* - Mandala to release fears in solar plexus **or** guided meditation to bring sunshine and warmth into solar plexus.

Behaviours: Can't focus on some tasks.
*Also links to* - brow chakra, aura
*Observations* - Ungrounded

*Balancing Mindful Activities* - Using the grounding mudra and focussing on sense of touch and the breath **or** use of weighted blankets.
*Additional Info* - Grounding mudra - Chapter 13

Emotions: Difficulty with loud/sudden sounds.
*Also links to* - solar plexus
*Observations* - Fear through stress response - on full alert.
*Balancing Mindful Activities* - Use the sense of sound (body/breath sound, outside sounds) to help with control and awareness. Create a meditation with imaginary golden earphones that filter out sounds **or** get child to shake off the stress, just as a dog or cat shakes after they've had a shock. Stamp feet and curl and relax toes.
*Additional Info* - Sense of sound - Chapter 9

Emotions: Dislikes any kind of change.
*Also links to* - solar plexus
*Observations* - Fear through stress response.
*Balancing Mindful Activities* - Use visual imagery to explain change – a seed growing to become a tree, the journey of a raindrop as it returns to the atmosphere. Relaxation and meditation practise using imagery above in imagination.

Emotions: Feeling calmer when stimulated through the senses (sound, touch, movement).
*Also links to* - solar plexus
*Balancing Mindful Activities* - Engage awareness of this to incorporate it into a form of meditation (using senses, movement through yoga and tactile items in meditation – e.g. feather, textiles, crystals/stones **or** self hugs – focussing on the feeling of touch. Heart centred hugs – aware of touch, energy of the heart and sense of touch.
*Additional Info* - Chapter 9 and Part 3

## Chakra: Sacral

**Relates to:** Connection to the world through family and friends

**Sacral Issues in Autism:**

- Emotional development is limited due to the internal priority of feeling safe and grounded (e.g; balancing the root chakra).

- Can pick up quickly on the emotional and mental states of others but causes them stress and not sure how to process this (child may either distance themselves/ignore others to cope or have a strong reaction to 'hidden' feelings/thought energy of others).

- Some have little self- imagination - e.g. limited in their own imagination, yet can tap into a 'universal imagination'.

- Difficulty in forming attachments to others - unable to access this emotionally or neurologically.

- Require rules to help them feel safe (organised) in a disorganised world. The ability to play and let go with their creativity is limited - the logical approach of rules help them feel safe. Being spontaneous is threatening (anything threatening engages the stress response).

- Fixation on TV and computer games which give a 2 dimensional view of the world. Perhaps the language seems clearer and less distorted by the energy of real people's thoughts and emotions. TV/games also offer 'rules' and a sense of control over life.

- This energy centre pairs with the throat chakra which affects our ability to talk, listen and interact socially and creatively.

Social Skills: Resistance to touch.
*Balancing Mindful Activities* - Similar to golden spacesuit, but using imagery of a golden wetsuit/dry suit so that it has closer contact to the skin offering more 'protection' of their energy field and able to cope with touch.
*Additional Info* - Chapter 5 and Chapter 8

Emotions: Emotions have a big impact.
*Observations* - Chemical and hormonal through stress response influencing the body.
*Balancing Mindful Activities* - Mindfully connecting them to emotions using colour, shape or numbers **or** using guided imagery to help them dissolve unhelpful or negative feelings (either offering them an image of the feeling melting in the sun like ice cream – or asking them to choose in their imagination how to dissolve the feeling).
*Additional Info* - Chapter 8

Social Skills: Unable to relate to another's feelings.
*Also links to* - solar plexus
*Balancing Mindful Activities* - Work with the heart centre – guiding meditation to help them connect to others **or** teach them about feelings through the sense of touch – using tactile information to help them relate (e.g; warm touch is happiness, cool touch is sadness).
*Additional Info* - Chapter 6

Social Skills: Difficult to keep friends.
*Also links to* - solar plexus
*Balancing Mindful Activities* - Breath work to help them control their reactions to others **or** colour meditation with the colour pink and green. Breathing in the colour, creating a bubble

around them and extending to others.
*Additional Info* - Breath work - Calm Kids Book, Colour meditation - Chapter 8

<u>Social Skills: Talks constantly about their own interests (usually focussed on 1 or 2 topics).</u>
*Also links to* - solar plexus and throat
*Balancing Mindful Activities* - Using the Namaste bow as a procedure to share. Use their interests as a theme for a guided meditation **or** breath work to help them practise this when someone else is talking **or** using the grounding mudra hand position and breathing in and out with the words 'peace' and 'love'.
*Additional Info* - Namaste bow - Chapter 14, Breath Work - Calm Kids Book, Grounding Mudra - Chapter 13

<u>Emotions: Inappropriate touching of self in public.</u>
*Also links to* - throat
*Observations* - Issues with feeling safe – this action connects to the root.
*Balancing Mindful Activities* - Engaging in breath work to recognise unsafe feelings and breathing for 1 minute before touching **or** bring in some colour breathing allowing them to choose the colour.
*Additional Info* - Breath Work - Calm Kids Book, Colour breathing - Chapter 8

<u>Social Skills: Responds to a social interact-tion but can't initiate</u>
*Also links to* - maybe throat
*Balancing Mindful Activities* - Engage them in the mindful practise of the labyrinth meditation (paper or walking) to help brain hemispheres connect.
*Additional Info* - Chapter 11

<u>Social Skills: Doesn't notice others</u>
*Also links to* - maybe throat
*Balancing Mindful Activities* - Using self bubble imagery to

imagine other people's bubbles - bubbles connecting.
*Additional Info* - Chapter 8

## Chakra: Solar Plexus

**Relates to:** Connection to the world with other people (school/work)

### Solar Plexus Issues in Autism:

- Unable to let go - this area becomes emotionally tight with fear and children struggle to let go. Digestive organs may be overwhelmed with bacteria combined with inability to let go and fear/stress response of the root chakra could lead to issues with bowel movements (constipation).

- Lack of balance - poor core strength can affect vestibular system (and vice versa) and sense of balance. This can negatively impact on their learning ability.

- Fear and emotions held in this chakra but lack of an effective feedback 'loop' between the brain makes it difficult to register this in the same way as others (in other words they don't notice the signals their body gives them).

- Once they are in the stress response, locked in and extremely difficult to release this (running, freezing or fighting).

Language Development: Uses a person's name excessively when speaking to them
*Observations* - Open to multiple inputs of information, they find it difficult to focus so trying to tune into person's energy by repeating their name.

*Balancing Mindful Activities* - Hand on core and hand on chest – as they say the person's name, notice where they feel that in their body (the vibration) and keep attention there as they speak.

Movement/Body: Clumsy – bumps into things/people
*Balancing Mindful Activities* - Practise the 'tree pose' in yoga to strengthen core and vestibular system.
*Additional Info* - Chapter 13

Movement/Body: Doesn't swing arms when walking
*Observations* - Activation of arms and legs is something we learn as babies as we crawl (connects hemispheres of brain).
*Balancing Mindful Activities* - Using energy techniques such as the cross crawl via Donna Eden's energy medicine **or** practising yoga.
*Additional Info* - Cross Crawl - Donna Eden, Yoga - Chapter 13

Movement/Body: Can't control bowel/bladder movement
*Observations* - Need to connect them to awareness of body.
*Balancing Mindful Activities* - With palms touching - ask them to focus on left hand then right (you may need to touch the hand they are to focus on. Can do this with eyes open at first then eyes closed and feeling the touch **or** practising yoga.
*Additional Info* - Yoga - Chapter 13

Behaviours: Extreme fear or phobia with no obvious reason
*Balancing Mindful Activities* - Emotional Freedom Technique (EFT) to help release fears and phobias. If children can't tolerate touch then surrogate tapping is better.
*Additional Info* - Level 2 Connected Kids programme

Behaviours: Verbal outbursts
*Balancing Mindful Activities* - Place hand on throat and one on core, focus on one hand then the other (perhaps using touch from parent). Using breath to help calm both areas **or** using the

hook up method.
*Additional Info* - Hook up method - Chapter 14

<u>Movement/Body: Constipation</u>
*Observations* - This could relate to food intolerances.
*Balancing Mindful Activities* - Tummy breathing, using a colour or image of sunshine filling core of body to relax it **or** yoga practise.
*Additional Info* - Yoga - Chapter 13

<u>Movement/Body: Excess flatulence, burping, sickness</u>
*Observations* - This could relate to food intolerances – important to keep a food diary.
*Balancing Mindful Activities* - Practise of meditation and yoga will help release stress from this area of the body.
*Additional Info* - Chapter 13

## Chakra: Heart Centre

**Relates to:** Connection to the world through feelings and emotional energy (love, compassion, forgiveness)

**Heart Centre Issues in Autism:**

- Sensitivity to energy (particularly the emotions of others) leaves them feeling that they are open to the 'pain' and 'grief' of the world's wounds. They can often feel like a pinball in a pinball machine due the impact of this energy from others. To survive and not be overwhelmed they may disconnect or distance themselves emotionally from others.

- Their heart centre expands their energy field (aura) for miles compared to the neurotypical human being whose energy field is normally 6 to 12 inches from the edge of the physical body. In most people it is only when we express love or when meditating that our energy field expands.

Emotions: Can't cope with too much verbal instruction.
*Also links to* - throat
*Observations* - Going into stress response and brain can't process information. Working with the breath (as it connects us to the heart centre and root as it is a physical action) helps children with autism to 'anchor' their awareness into the present moment and engage with the breath.
*Balancing Mindful Activities* - Adults to 'check in' to their own mindful awareness when speaking to the child **or** teach child to focus on breath with 'peace' and 'love' when being given instructions to help process. Use their favourite number/image with awareness in a breath meditation (repeating to themselves silently) then through sound – saying the word with awareness and how it makes them feel.
*Additional Info* - 'check in' - Chapter 3, focus on breath - Calm Kids book

Emotions: Either becomes upset or zones out if being scolded.
*Also links to* - crown and ears
*Balancing Mindful Activities* - Adults to 'check in' to their own mindful awareness when speaking to the child **or** use the 'angry sock' method to help them release stress **or** breath work helps them to 'weigh down' their awareness and energy into this moment so that they can more easily process emotions (and start to feel safe).
*Additional Info* - 'check in' - Chapter 3, 'angry sock' - Part 3, focus on breath - Calm Kids book

Emotions: Needs alone time to release frustration.
*Also links to* - crown and brow
*Balancing Mindful Activities* - Use of a mandala to release frustration mindfully **or** the 'angry sock' method
*Additional Info* - Mandala - Chapter 10, 'angry sock' - Part 3

Emotions: Desires comfort 'things' (rock, string).

*Also links to* - aura

*Balancing Mindful Activities* - Use this item as a tool for a mindful touch meditation to explore the senses **or** using the breath with physical objects (windmills, feathers or balloons) gives them a physical connection to the breath and their bodies **or** using grounding images and words (tree, anchor, mountain, planet or rock) is another way to ground the breath **or** invite them to imagine and breathe in a 'golden breath'. In energy terms, gold is a very protective colour and this can help them feel safe and supported. Their 'golden body' creates a grounding effect that helps them cope with the world.

*Additional Info* - Use the item as a tool - Calm Kids book, Using the breath - Part 3, Using grounding words - Calm Kids Book

## Chakra: Throat Centre

**Relates to:** Connection to the world through communication (hearing, speaking and thinking)

**Throat Centre Issues in Autism:**

- They understand but they lack the ability to communicate in the way we do. I believe that they are communicating telepathically and become very frustrated with us when we don't hear or understand them. They have evolved beyond the need to communicate using the physical body, but we (neurotypicals) still rely on this.

- Grunting/noises – with a different way of communicating that we can't connect with, they then have to rely on the older ways (eg using their physical body) to communicate. Imagine that in the Western world we go back to using a horse and cart instead of a car for travel; it feels heavy, clumsy and limited. This is how it feels for children with autism who are trying to communicate with us using the older physical structures of the body. The use of technology (typing on a keyboard) has helped many with autism to illustrate that they are highly intelligent but have limited physical speech.

- Hearing issues - it isn't that children with autism choose to ignore us when we speak to them, but for them it can sound distant, like a foreign language or so imperceptible that they simply don't hear the tone or the sound; it is as if their hearing is attuned to a different frequency and wavelength to the one we speak.

Language Development: Speech is unusually loud or quiet
*Balancing Mindful Activities* - Teach them the 'ocean sounding breath'
*Additional Info* - Chapter 9

Language Development: Speech started early then stopped for a period
*Balancing Mindful Activities* - Sound meditation with vowels but moving around the musical scale and encouraging mindful sounds as each one connects.
*Additional Info* - Chapter 9

Behavious: Causing self injury – biting or banging head
*Observations* - Children may be trying to control as feel out of control due to stress.
*Balancing Mindful Activities* - Working with tuning forks, singing bowls and making sounds through the chanting can be a way for them to help attune their energy to our wavelength.
*Additional Info* - Chapter 9

Movement/Body: Appears to have hearing problems but checks out okay
*Observations* - Your own meditation practise helps you tune in

to your child.

*Balancing Mindful Activities* - Adult 'check in' – listen to how you say the child's name. Place your hand on your chest and say their name mindfully and feel the vibration in your body. Extend that vibration to them as you speak.

*Additional Info* - Chapter 3

Social Skills: Responds to a social interaction but can't initiate

*Also links to* - sacral

*Balancing Mindful Activities* - 'peace and love' breath to help them reduce anxiety.

*Additional Info* - Calm Kids book

Emotions: In appropriate touching of self in public

*Also links to* - sacral

*Balancing Mindful Activities* - Holding the grounding hand mudra and practising this. Holding it for 3 breaths before the urge to touch **or** using the hook up method.

*Additional Info* - Grounding hand mudra - Chapter 13, Hook up method - Chapter 14

Social Skills: Honest comments that can be inappropriate

*Also links to* - brow

*Balancing Mindful Activities* - 'peace and love' breath to help them with self control.

*Additional Info* - Calm Kids book

Emotions: Unable to tolerate certain foods, colours or way displayed on plate

*Also links to* - brow

*Observations* - Children 'tune in' to the energy of the food.

*Balancing Mindful Activities* - Practise a gratitude meditation before eating (like saying 'grace') except mindfully aware of journey of food to plate. For meat, thanking animal for their energy.

*Additional Info* - Chapter 6

School: Exceptional high skills in some areas, low in others
*Also links to* - brow
*Balancing Mindful Activities* - Amygdala hold of head (also spend time holding ears with hands) – can be self-hold or parents holding head.
*Additional Info* - Chapter 12

Language Development: Echolalia (makes sounds when listening) - repeating last words several times
*Also links to* - some brow
*Observations* - This is a comfort technique. People often say 'uh huh' when listening.
*Balancing Mindful Activities* - Mindfully listening to sounds they make in their head and noticing silence when no sound.
*Additional Info* - Chapter 9

Language Development: Unable to understand directional terms (eg: before or after)
*Also links to* - brow and crown
*Observations* - Feelings of stress interfere with ability to absorb information.
*Balancing Mindful Activities* - Practise breath awareness so they can do this mindfully when listening **or** the hook up method.
*Additional Info* - Breath - Calm Kids book, Hook up method - Chapter 14

Emotions: Sensitivity (or lack of sensitivity to sounds or other senses)
*Also links to* - crown and ears
*Balancing Mindful Activities* - Golden spacesuit meditation
*Additional Info* - Chapter 5

Language Development: Sensitivity (or lack of sensitivity to sounds or other senses)
*Also links to* - ears
*Observations* - They 'hear' the emotional energy in others so they copy this.

*Balancing Mindful Activities* - Practising sound meditations with the vowels.
*Additional Info* - Chapter 9

Language Development: Finds it difficult to whisper
*Also links to* - ears
*Balancing Mindful Activities* - Practising sound meditations with the vowels.
*Additional Info* - Chapter 9

School: Short attention span
*Also links to* - crown
*Balancing Mindful Activities* - The more they practise meditation to reduce stress, this will improve.

School: Can't follow directions
*Also links to* - crown
*Balancing Mindful Activities* - Golden sunshine meditation – standing under the sun and it flows around and through them.

## Chakra: Brow

**Relates to:** Connection with the internal world through our thoughts and perceptions of the outer world

**Brow Issues in Autism:**

- Overload of information - unable to cope with the information of the senses, the brain is overloaded and potentially affects the brain's normal development as it experiences stress.

- Dominant Brain - some children can be more right-brained (tend to be imaginative/creative) while others are more left-brained (logical and non-emotional) - the 2 hemispheres of the brain are not connecting effectively.

- Overwhelmed – in some cases, children with autism have to cope with unimaginable life situations. Imagine that you walk outside but instead of hearing a few birds singing you could hear all the birds in your city! Or that your sense of smell was so acute you could smell dog faeces in the street, cooking smells streets away or body odour. Head banging may be an attempt through pain to distract away from this intensity.

- Root chakra effect - being overwhelmed in the brow and crown chakras can make children less grounded.

- The hippocampus (which can be regarded as the 'filing clerk' of the brain, helping to place short-term information into our long-term memory for future retrieval) can shrink in size when under stress - it's as if the 'clerk' is on holiday. This may explain how some children are unable to remember or follow instructions.

Behaviours: Obsessions with objects or ideas
*Observations* - Desire to feel 'safe'.
*Balancing Mindful Activities* - Walking meditation to ground energy. Combine with labyrinth to help brain hemispheres connect.
*Additional Info* - Chapter 11

Behaviours: Compulsive behaviour patterns
*Balancing Mindful Activities* - Breath meditation of 'peace and love' to help reduce anxiety **or** for those children who like their heads to be touched, head massage or the amygdala hold can help filter out the 'noise' of their thoughts.
*Additional Info* - Breath meditation - Calm Kids book, head massage - Chapter 12 and Chapter 13

Behaviours: Fascination with rotation
*Balancing Mindful Activities* - Bring this mindfully into

meditation while connecting their awareness to the sense of touch, breath, sound, body etc.

Behaviours: Repetitive play
*Observations* - This is a comfort activity to reduce stress.
*Balancing Mindful Activities* - Bring attention to the senses as they play – using this with mindful awareness to reduce anxiety in body.

Social Skills: Can't read facial expression or body language
*Balancing Mindful Activities* - Using emotion charts to teach them visually about different emotions. Then guiding them to sense emotions in their body through colour, sounds, shape.

Movement/Body: Irregular sleep pattern
*Balancing Mindful Activities* - Practising meditation can help to regulate sleep. Using progressive muscle relaxation at bed-time.
*Additional Info* - Calm Kids book

Behaviours: Quotes movies or video games
*Balancing Mindful Activities* - Create a guided meditation around the theme of their favourite movie/video game **or** using the words in a sound meditation to connect to their body.
*Additional Info* - using the words - Chapter 9

Behaviours: Gross motor skills are behind peers in their development. (running, riding a bike)
*Observations* - Links to reduced neural cross connection between the brain hemispheres.
*Balancing Mindful Activities* - Practising yoga, walking, labyrinth meditation **or** reverse cycling (lying on back with legs in the air and cycling).
*Additional Info* - yoga, walking, labyrinth - Chapter 13 and Chapter 11

Behaviours: Fine motor skills behind peers - writing, tying shoelaces

*Balancing Mindful Activities* - Using the paper labyrinth meditation **or** practising 'peace and love' breath meditation when trying to learn new skills.
*Additional Info* - labyrinth - Chapter 11, breath - Calm Kids book

School: Fine motor skills behind peers - writing, tying shoelaces
*Observations* - For those children who like their heads to be touched, head massage can help filter out the 'noise' of their thoughts.
*Balancing Mindful Activities* - Cross crawl energy technique **or** labyrinth meditation
*Additional Info* - Cross crawl - Donna Eden, labyrinth - Chapter 11

Behaviours: Lots of collections
*Also links to* - root
*Balancing Mindful Activities* - Make these a 'theme' of the guided meditation to engage their interest in meditation practise.

Movement/Body: Seizures
*Also links to* - crown
*Balancing Mindful Activities* - Amygdala hold
*Additional Info - Chapter 12*

Social Skills: Little or no eye contact
*Also links to* - crown
*Balancing Mindful Activities* - 'Peace and love' breath meditation **or** mudras for grounding
*Additional Info* - breath - Calm Kids book, mudras - Chapter 13

Crown and the aura imbalances have already been addressed in the above charts. The practise of meditation and these mindfulness techniques will help their energy to come into balance, reduce stress and anxiety and help children with autism process the world around them. These techniques are not a 'cure'. They are a set of life skills that these children can use to help them cope with life.

## Chakra: Crown

**Relates to:** Connecting with the universe of information/energy

**Crown Issues in Autism:**

- Metaphorically speaking, the crown is like the door to our world. Imagine your child's body is a house, and the crown is the front door. Autistic children don't appear to have a door - in fact, the whole wall that should contain the door is absent. Unlike most people, they have access to the universal 'brain' thus they can have an incredible attention to detail or information. Meditation helps to calm and ground the body, perhaps helping children to combine this 'access' with more balance in the rest of their physical body to help them facilitate their way through life in a calmer way. Many have suggested that the geniuses in our time (Leonardo de Vinci and Einstein) were on the autistic spectrum.

## Centering thought for your personal meditation practice

Which of your child's energy centres do you feel are out of balance?

## PART 3 - CASE STUDIES

### What we learned from kids with special needs

The case studies are an important part of this book to show you how this heart centred approach to teaching meditation really works. They help us show you how each journey and each child is different.

Following an online application in the spring of 2013, we recruited 30 families/groups from around the world. Through the selection process we chose 15 who could commit their time and energy. The published results are based on 6 families/groups who demonstrated a range of health issues and who practised the mindful activities presented in this book.

Once we had selected the children, I invited a group of 'Connected Kids' tutors to assist; we used the heart centre meditation to help develop intuitive solutions that the family could try. From these findings, I would do further research to inform and develop our 'plan'.

## Our main focus...

There were two recurring issues:

- helping the parents/carers/educators feel calmer and able to cope,

- helping children to find ways to manage their emotions and reduce the effects of stress.

Following this preparation and research, I presented the family with a range of mindful ideas that they could select from depending on their interests, lifestyle and experience; if I suggested yoga and the adult didn't have experience of this then I would signpost them to online resources and videos.

The themes for the meditations were also optional, and we encouraged parents and professionals to develop or change them. We encouraged the adults to 'tune in' and trust their intuition rather than just follow our heart-centered suggestions.

## Embracing intuitive solutions...

The heart centre energy holds the intuitive intelligence that inspires these creative solutions. (This is explained in Chapter 6 - 'Connecting to heart centre intelligence' which includes the heart centre meditation for you to try.)

When working intuitively from the heart centre, it's important to acknowledge but switch off the logical mind. This helps us access more creative solutions; the analytical mind can often hinder the creative process.

## What we discovered...

1. Children with special needs may be in a high state of stress and that meditation and mindful activities gives them some respite from the triggers that create this.

2. Each child is unique and requires a bespoke, mindful activity to help him feel calm, connected and centered.

3. Each time we deliver a mindful activity we have the opportunity to 'tune in' to the needs of the children we are teaching. Working <u>without</u> a meditation script or someone else's meditation provides the adult with the freedom to engage with what feels right for that child.

4. Mindful activities need to engage the interest of children/young people; choosing a theme which appeals to their energy and their interests.

5. The expected attention span doesn't necessarily relate to age when working with kids who have additional support needs. It was important to start small with regular practise and gently build up their concentration skills. With practise, their ability to focus improves considerably.

6. With regular practise, positive results were seen within 3 to 4 weeks.

7. The approach to teaching mindful activities has to grow organically; not simply sticking to the same routine because it was initially effective.

8. Children with special needs, in particular autism, usually require a movement-based mindful activity (such as yoga) to help balance their energy before they can then approach a technique that requires focus and concentration while seated.

9. Some children on the autistic spectrum lack the ability to use their imagination. In these circumstances it was important to bring in meditation props for sensory input; objects that they could touch and see as part of (or before) the sitting meditation.

10. Teaching meditation from the heart centre helps us move beyond the limitations of logic and provides the opportunity to tune in to the needs of children to develop inspired and creative solutions.

11. The 'amygdala hold' is particularly effective for children who can't switch off their minds or who have sleep issues.

12. The emotional and mental state of the main caregiver or educator has a huge influence on the energy of the child;

if the parents are calm, the children sense this and have more potential to feel calm.

## A final word...

When we started to teach kids with special needs how to meditate, I had a hunch that it could work but no proof. I had a sense that kids would benefit mentally, emotionally and physically and wanted to see if it was possible. During this experience, these children have taught me that they can do it and, yes, they really benefit from learning meditation.

I sincerely hope that this book (and the following information) inspires you to develop bespoke, mindful activities for your kids. But remember - it's a journey you share together. Allow them teach you... as you teach them.

# Annabel, (aged 7) and Mum, Megan

## Presenting symptoms

Annabel is suffering from anxiety attacks. She is a 'thinker' but it had never before stopped her from doing the things she loved. Now, she has separation anxiety from her mum, and often feels nauseous when at school; school assembly can be overwhelming for her. Megan says she cannot leave her with a babysitter any more.

A school bully has knocked her confidence. She's witnessed some home tension and arguments. She gets angry if her plans have to change - screaming, crying and stomping her feet.

Parent's intention - Megan's intention for her daughter, *"I am hoping the meditation will help her to calm down, ground herself and find a new self-confidence to help her cope or get over her anxiety."*

## The Journey...

Heart centre meditation - to tune into Annabel's energy for insights to develop bespoke mindful activities.

Adult support - mindful breathing; to help with tension in the home I suggested that Megan practise some mindful breath awareness to help her to feel calmer in tense situations (see below for the mindfulness script).

## Mindful activities suggested for Annabel:

Yoga

The warrior (this develops compassion and forgiveness) and fish (helps release anger) postures.

I suggested daily practise (or a minimum of 3 times per week) to help discharge the stress of school. To encourage Annabel to feel it was a shared experience (and not simply her mum telling her what to do) I suggested that they take turns in leading each other through the yoga postures, before practising together.

Meditations

*Stars meditation*; guide her to imagine that she is holding a gold and a silver star in each hand. The twinkles get brighter and brighter with each in and out breath. While holding the stars, guide her to imagine that smaller stars start to float out of them and around her body, for protection and peace. Slowly bring these stars back to the two larger gold and silver stars in each hand. (Suggestion - mention feelings like warmth and calmness as you guide her).

*Sunshine meditation*; ask her to imagine that she has sunshine in her tummy as if she's swallowed a part of the sun. Guide her to imagine the feeling of this sunshine as a warm, light sensation that spreads around her body. Ask her to imagine that there is a big smile painted on her tummy and combine this with the warmth of the sunshine.

The star meditation would engage awareness of her left and right sides of her body (in her imagination) as well as tapping into Annabel's love of being creative. The sunshine meditation can help relieve any tightness and tension in the solar plexus where children can hold anger.

Amygdala Soother

To reduce built up stress, I suggested that Megan demonstrated to her daughter how to massage her temples in a forward direction (towards the brow); finger tips on either side of the head, in the temples area, and massage forward while focussing on the breath. I encouraged frequent practise and particularly if stressed. This method would engage the amygdala (as explained in Chapter 12 - 'Calming the nervous system').

This would be an easy way to move Annabel's brain out of the reactive stress response so she could engage the executive functions of her brain (pre-frontal cortex).

Affirmations

To help improve self-esteem, Annabel was invited to use the affirmation "I am beautiful" at any time she chose and especially in meditation. To enhance its effect, Annabel could also hug herself. To help them relax into it, both parent and child would practise some mindful breathing. Focussing on the breath but initially breathing in/out the words (silently) "I am beautiful". Following this, to reach a point where Annabel could repeat it out loud.

The affirmation would help Annabel feel good about herself (after being bullied). The hug would engage the heart centre and saying the words out loud engages the throat chakra.

The 'angry sock' Mindful Activity

To release 'stored' emotion in the throat - invite her to draw a picture or write the name of whoever makes her feel angry or upset, and stick it on a door or wall. Take some rolled up socks and let her vociferously throw the socks at the picture, encouraging her to grunt or shout while throwing. Annabel might feel frustrated and this is a safe way to help release these tensions.

Mindful Activities Created by Family/Annabel

- Sitting cross-legged, holding hands and concentrating on the breath.

- Blowing away thoughts that pop into busy or worried minds.

- Practise throwing away worries by imagining throwing stones in the water, and saying at the end of each session: "Just for today, I will not be worried. Just for today, I will not be angry. Just for today, I will love all."

## Feedback (from Megan)

*"I have practised (almost) daily meditation/breath work, some by myself and some with Annabel. We have had great fun doing a lot of blowing and laughing at the start of the sessions.*

*Going to school is easier. I have spoken to her about her feelings and the colours quite regularly. It's always black and in the throat when she gets angry - probably quite an apt way of describing angry feelings.*

*She has started yoga classes which are great as they include a bit of everything - relaxation, meditation, yoga moves and positions, yoga "ethics", health benefits, massaging techniques etc. She is very calm when she comes out.*

*Annabel was upset the other night about feeling excluded from school. After we had a good, calm chat about life and friendships, we did some breathing together, breathing in bright, warm happiness and breathing out negative, black things in our life. She was asleep within a couple of minutes. I think it's a combination of being used to the whole concept of breath calming us down and practising it in her yoga class and at home.*

*My big commitment is to either do a spot of yoga or mindfulness or meditation every day, not just whenever I find the time. We seem to talk about plans more than what we have actually done, but we are doing what we can to make [meditation] more a part of our daily lives. Your tips have all really helped, and we will continue to try out different ideas."*

## Conclusion

Reading the initial case study notes, I could sense that there was a slight power struggle between daughter and mum. This inspired my suggestion that Megan and her daughter take turns in leading the meditation and the yoga postures so that they could help each other to relax. If children feel they are being 'controlled' they normally resist! By taking turns to 'lead', it would help both to share the experience.

It seemed likely that there had been a build-up of chronic stress (bully, home tension etc) in Annabel who was holding in a lot of feelings she didn't know how to process or express. This causes children stress and all the suggested mindful activities were to help her release this.

The mindful activity was important for Megan as I could tell from her emails that there had been some home tensions causing everyone stress. Children pick up on this. It helps enormously if the adult can practise mindfulness to feel calmer as this helps their children.

Initially, teaching your kids meditation may seem like climbing a mountain but it is simply a case of one foot in front of the other. I try to encourage people to find normal day to day activities that they can incorporate some mindfulness with their children so that they don't feel they have to squeeze another task into an overflowing schedule.

## Mindful Breathing for adults

*Notice the breath*
*Notice the breath inside body (in the chest)*
*Notice thoughts/emotions - then let go*
*Notice the breath*
*Notice the body for tension/pain - then let go*
*Notice the breath*

In order to accept/change strong emotions/thoughts or relax the body we need to be aware there was tension in the first place. To do this you can practise mindful breathing throughout the day. If you can practise this you will learn how to be relaxed and calm when spending time with your children.

Try to practise this (it will take 30 to 60 seconds) frequently throughout the day. Here are some tips.

- When you notice a thought, simply acknowledge it but let it go and come back to the breath.

- Take your attention to the area of the chest (heart centre) as you notice the breath and try to feel the energy of your breath here. It helps to shift your awareness out of your thoughts.

- Similar to noticing thoughts, notice the physical tension but let it go from your awareness and come back to the breath.

- Stick a few reminders around your environment with the word 'breathe'.

Try to use day to day activities as triggers; below is an example but it's not exhaustive and choose things that will 'trigger' your awareness to notice the breath.

- Before you brush your teeth

- Standing in the shower

- Waiting at a traffic light

- Waiting for a kettle to boil

- Before taking a drink of water

- Sitting at your computer

- Every time you check Facebook/Twitter!

- Before you start to eat

- Waiting for your children to arrive back from school

- Whilst children are playing or doing homework

- Waiting in a line at the supermarket/shop

- Whilst reading/watching TV

If you find that you forget to practise and only manage once a day or when you remember, try not to judge and criticise yourself. Instead, congratulate yourself for remembering!

# Jaden (aged 9) and his mum, Renee

## Presenting symptoms

Jaden has OCD (Obsessive Compulsive Disorder); symptoms include excessive hand washing and wiping; night-time fears; general anxieties and lack of focus (executive function) issues. He likes to call these 'his fears' and 'his rituals'.

He is highly intelligent. He tends to be very logical and precise, but still uses a lot of imagination. He can be impulsive and has a deep need to be totally honest. He can focus on books but has little sense of time.

He becomes stressed if rushed. He is a perfectionist and a very black-and-white thinker; he sometimes has anger issues when something does not go his way. Anger is a 'power' emotion - he likes to stay stuck in anger. Food can also cause issues.

Parent's intention - Renee's intention for teaching Jaden meditation, *"I want to help him get the skills that he will need to move through life with calm and focus."*

## The Journey...

Heart centre meditation - to tune into Jaden's energy for insights which led to the following suggestions.

Adult support - Mindful breathing and grounding - Renee and partner to try mindful breathing to reduce their anxiety - especially around Jaden. Renee to practise grounding to get out of head and into her body (e.g. walking in nature, yoga - she is a yoga teacher).

## Mindful activities suggested for Jaden:

Yoga

The mountain pose (for grounding) and the fish pose (to release anger). See Chapter 13 - *'Yoga, mudras and massage'*.

Meditations

*Airplane meditation*; invite your child to imagine they are in an aeroplane which is flying upwards. In the back of the plane are boxes and bags that represent worries and feelings. Invite him to imagine throwing these out of the plane and feel the plane get lighter. Once he has released all or as many as he can, the plane brings him back to earth.

*Shield meditation*; invite your child to imagine he has a blue shield; ask him to choose the construction, size and material - perhaps something from outer space (one of Jaden's interests). Invite him to imagine bringing this across his tummy at school or whenever he is in a place or situation where he feels afraid.

*Dragon meditation*; guide him to visualise a dragon in his tummy (solar plexus). This is his power centre. When he feeds the dragon positive words, his tummy is happy and relaxed. It's magical, as the dragon can eat up his unhappy feelings. His dragon is with him at school, and when he thinks of a certain word (which he can choose) he feels protected.

Mindful activities created by family/Jaden -

- *Petting the cat mindfully*

- *Listening to sounds in nature*

- *Deep relaxation*

- *Chanting 'Om'*

## Feedback (from Renee)

*"He loved the airplane meditation. He ended up exploding the packages that he dumped off the plane. He made statements like "Mom, is meditation magic because my anger just evaporated?" so he is noticing, like I am, that he is starting to pause and make new choices.*

*Jaden asks for meditation every school morning. He likes to light the candle and asks for something to focus on. He likes to tell me what happened for him.*

*He shocked me again last night when he was tired and throwing a big tantrum in the car and then suddenly chose to turn it off. This was not accessible to him in the past—if he got caught up in a tantrum it would have lasted for hours and hours as he grabs onto one thought and won't let it go, and just goes in deeper and deeper.*

*I was very proud of the days he petted the cat because he chose to do something very uncharacteristic (he'll pet the cat, but not usually in such a focused way or for so long). He liked that petting the cat was meditative and he stuck with it for half an hour or more.*

*Jaden seemed to really enjoy the airplane meditation. He had used it for dealing with a bully (giving the bully a parachute) and for his anger and fears.*

*Jaden had a resurgence in fears after a few weeks of being fear-free. At night, he started insisting that he was hearing sounds. One night we found real sources of sounds... he was able to giggle about it and let it go. This was a big shift for him."*

## Conclusion

Renee's commitment to yoga and meditation supported her commitment to teaching Jaden. As a result, they made some great progress.

The meditations helped him release anger and protect the area of the solar plexus which (as an energy centre) links to control issues and self-esteem.

Jaden was starting to practise meditation through choice (eg; petting cat)

Progress was like a chess match - trying one 'move', then waiting to see what happened before trying another. We noticed that Renee was starting to trust her own intuition and developing mindful activities to teach Jaden.

# Adam, (aged 13) and Grandmother, Barbara

## Presenting symptoms

Since infancy Adam experienced Beckwith-Wiedemann syndrome; presenting issues with his body and organ development and he has a higher chance of cancerous or non-cancerous tumours in childhood.

He has Lennox syndrome which causes behavioural problems. He has limited speech but can comprehend. He demonstrates the behaviour of a five or six year old. He can't read but can count from one to 10.

He has physical disabilities - unable to stand straight or walk. Medication is affecting is sleep patterns.

Grandparent's intention - Barbara's intention for teaching Adam meditation, "I would like to try meditation for special children because he needs something that can help him to control his behaviour."

## The Journey...

Heart centre meditation - to tune into Adam's energy for insights to develop bespoke mindful activities.

Adult support - Mindful breathing (it wasn't possible to invite other members of the family to try this). Barbara taught yoga so I felt she would find it easy to practise.

## Mindful activities suggested for Adam:

Mindful breathing videos

The videos use a combination of imagery (a cartoon of a butterfly opening and closing its wings) to represent the 'in' and 'out' breath while the voiceover counts to 3 for each breath. Barbara and Adam's first language is Spanish.

I suggested that she invite Adam to watch the breathing videos and practice; encouraging him to place his hand on his chest so that he could feel the breath in his chest. If he couldn't do this, I suggested that Barbara place her hand on his chest.

Regular practice is important so I suggested that Adam practise this once a day (or more if he enjoyed it). To help him feel grounded during this, to ensure his feet were flat on the ground as he watched the video, or he could sit on the ground. Initially he could watch the video with eyes open, then repeat while listening with eyes closed.

Spanish: http://www.youtube.com/watch?v=q75yIzNuYNI
English: http://www.youtube.com/watch?v=nL7tA_Rf5_s

Yoga

Adam would benefit from yoga that helped balance his heart chakra. With his limited movement, it was important for Barbara to choose the poses he could do. Ideally, he would practise yoga once a day for seven days. During the practice, I asked Barbara to help Adam focus on the heart chakra with his breath; to think of his breath going in and out of his chest. Working on the heart centre helps to release feelings of anger.

Yoga: welcome to the sun (opening the heart centre)

This is a gentle movement that works well at opening the heart chakra. It is usually practised while standing, but it would work equally well with a child sitting in a chair. A child with very restricted movement could be supported by an adult's hands into the posture. This yoga pose is gentler for the heart; it can bring a feeling of balance.

Breathing in - invite your child to bring his hands together with palms touching, rounding the shoulders and tucking his chin down (suggestion - it is a quiet time and the moon is out).

Breathing out - ask him to imagine that the sun comes out as he brings his arms behind him like beautiful wings (as far as is comfortable); his palms are open, his shoulders opened up. He imagines opening his heart centre to the sky and his face lifted to the sun. As his wings open up to the sun he can sense the warmth on them (suggestion – noticing the colours in his wings).

Then invite him to move gently from one (breathing in) pose to the other (breathing out).

Meditations

*A balloon meditation:* invite him to imagine holding balloons; each balloon represents something he feels angry about. Guide him to notice the colour of the balloons. Ask him to let go of the balloons and watch them till they disappear. Help him notice (in his body) how he feels after the balloons are gone.

Mindful activities created by family/Adam

- Sphinx Pose,

- Bidalasana (Cat Pose),

- Supta Baddha Konasana (Supine Bound Angle),

- Matsyasana (Fish Pose).

All these yoga postures help to open the heart chakra. Barbara had guided Adam to try a yoga video online
http://www.youtube.com/watch?v=SP5p1gLUOHI.

## Feedback (from Barbara)

*"Adam has been doing the breath exercise that you sent us. He manages it very well. He practised breathing with the video.*

*He enjoys practising yoga and the video. I feel very comfortable teaching him. I think he feels relaxed. The butterfly video has helped him.*

*Adam has had excellent behaviour for three weeks. He has practised yoga and meditation better each day. He breathes better, too. Thank you so much.*

*Adam was violent when he got angry, but with regular meditation he has become peaceful and can sleep better. Since we started, we have taken many good things from this approach that has helped him for his mind, his behaviour and his health."*

## Conclusion

The breathing video felt important;

- to help Adam focus on his breath using counting and imagery,

- with the breath as an anchor, Adam could learn how to help his body to relax,

- balancing the breath helps to reduce the effects of long term stress.

Placing his hand on his chest would help Adam to connect his breath to his body; anchoring it into his body. If he sat and watched the video whilst connected to the ground, this would support his sense of feeling grounded and safe.

The yoga poses suggested by Barbara are easy to find through searching on the internet. Barbara chose different yoga poses from my suggestions as she intuitively knew what would be more suited to his abilities. It is important for the person teaching mindful activities like yoga to trust this intuition and their common sense.

I suggested a theme for a meditation to help Adam release some of the anger he had been feeling; the balloon meditation is a great way to help children imagine a feeling in each balloon and using the imagination to release the balloon (and feeling) into the sky. The colours children choose for this can relate to the chakra system. It is important to guide children to check in with how they feel after a meditation so that they can notice any difference in their thoughts/emotions.

## Evan, (aged 9) and Mum, Donna

### Presenting symptoms

Evan was diagnosed with high functioning autism (2008) and hyperacusis (2009) - the latter is a sensitivity to certain sounds; hand dryers, dogs and babies crying or the school bell.

He never sits still - always running backwards and forwards. He talks constantly or makes random noises (if not in conversation). He has a wide range of vocabulary but apparently has a lack of comprehension for his age group.

Evan is creative and has a good imagination for topics that interest him. He can be quite sensitive and cries at sad films. He takes medication for constipation and attends a homeopathic clinic, speech therapy and occupational therapy.

Parent's intention - Donna's intention for her son, *"I would like to find a tool that can support Evan and provide a tool for him to use as he gets older."*

### The Journey...

Heart centre meditation - to tune into Evan's energy to help develop bespoke mindful activities.

Adult support - mindful breathing; any parent with a child on the autistic spectrum could be expected to have a high level of stress. I suggested that Donna try the mindful breath practice (see previous case study) to help her feel calmer. This would help her feel more relaxed when trying the techniques (and perhaps more likely to adapt them intuitively if required). Donna had joined a mindfulness group to help her learn more about meditation and to help her relax and reduce stress.

## Mindful activities suggested for Evan:

Yoga

Spinal twists and crab pose (an internal 'massage') and rocking on toes (for grounding). I encouraged Donna to practise this with Evan daily/3 times a week.

I felt these postures would help Evan prepare for school and reduce stress. The spinal twists and the crab pose help the body by massaging and stretching out the intestines, perhaps helping his bowel movements and reducing stress in this part of his body.

Meditations

*Star meditation*; invite your child to imagine a star shining in his belly button. The star is shining into his solar plexus and down to his feet. You hold his feet, and he holds his belly button area. While doing this, guide him to relax every part of his body. (Suggestion - ask him to imagine the starlight shining into different parts of his body).

The intention of this meditation was to help Evan connect his awareness with his body (through noticing his feet); helping him feel more grounded and balanced. The focus on his solar plexus would help his physical body to relax. My theory about children who are constipated is that their high state of stress contributes to tension and this part of the body becomes 'locked' making it difficult for them to release their bowels without straining. As meditation helps the body to relax both physically and emotionally, the body can bring itself into balance and encourage regular bowel movements.

*Drum beat meditation*; using a drum (preferably with a soft skin/soft beat drum). Use the palms of your hands to beat alternately while he notices where he feels the sound in his body. A recording of rhythmical drum beats could be used instead.

The drum beat meditation combines the sense of touch and sound - helping to ground his energy. If a child likes this sound, it can be soothing. Native Indian Drums are said to create a sound that resonates with the root chakra and are very grounding.

Amygdala hold

This can help reduce high stress levels (full instructions are in Chapter 12 - 'Calming the nervous system'). This 'head hold' could bring some deep relaxation while helping Donna to simultaneously practise a moment of mindfulness.

Mindful activities created by family/Evan:

- Meditating as a family

- Bedtime meditation - deep breathing while listening to nature sounds (a phone app)

- Deep breathing at onset of verbal/physical tics.

## Feedback (from Donna)

*"On the first night, I tried to lead a meditation about water to link to the sound (on the phone app) he had chosen, but Evan told me to stop talking and was asleep within five minutes (this usually takes 30 minutes after reading time). We have played the sound (app) throughout the night for the past week and Evan has slept soundly and stayed in bed throughout, other than on three nights.*

*We have also noticed a reduction in random running back and forth in the house.*

*I have been happy with all exercises provided. We didn't make any adjustments to the yoga practise, but I encouraged Evan to practise the spinal twists and rocking on toes outwith the home sessions to help his coordination, keep his mind focused, and to keep him out of trouble at school or if he needs a movement break. We have been told that Evan may have short-term auditory processing issues, so hopefully the yoga focus might help.*

*I love the amygdala hold. I use it every time I put Evan to bed, and sometimes just when he is sitting beside me. My husband also uses one hand on the back of Evan's neck, as he finds it difficult to use both hands. Evan has tried a few times to do this on his own, but it will take more practise.*

*The hold settles him really quickly, sometimes within a minute. I just hold his head when I know he has gone to sleep - his breathing is steady and he looks so peaceful. It feels like, if I take my hands away, he will lose what is probably the least anxious time of his day."*

## Conclusion

With regular practise, guided by Donna's intuition, Evan was learning life skills that would help him in different stressful life situations (e.g. school).

Donna had made the commitment to learn mindfulness which would be very important in reducing her stress levels while demonstrating to Evan her own personal commitment to meditation (kids can question why they should practise meditation if no-one else is doing it).

Although I offered a number of different suggestions, this case study clearly demonstrates the importance t of the parent choosing an approach that they feel comfortable with which was clearly illustrated by Donna applying the amygdala hold; this was empowering for both mother and son.

# James, (aged 4) and Mum, Vanessa

## Presenting symptoms

James has no confirmed diagnosis yet there is a communication disorder and possible ASD (Autistic Spectrum Disorder), but his paediatrician is not sure he meets all the criteria. He lashes out physically when he is upset and consequently struggles to build relationships with his peers.

James is very excitable and struggles to listen. At home he looks for the next stimulant though he can sit still in nursery. He has a sensitivity to sudden loud noises and dislikes busy places. He becomes easily frustrated as his fine motor skills are poor and he struggles to pay attention to a task as he is so easily distracted.

He doesn't like change, whether it is a new teacher or furniture moving in the house.

He will do imaginative play, usually initiated by his brother, and he shows imagination through demonstrating fears.

He takes medication as he suffers regularly from rectal prolapse. His speech and language therapist helped create a visual timetable and social stories.

Parent's intention - Vanessa's intention for teaching her son meditation, *"I love my son, but he can be very challenging. Family fun can be difficult and he is always so sad not to be invited to parties etc. I would like to help him function more comfortably in the world we live in."*

## The Journey...

Heart centre meditation - to help tune into James' energy for insights to create bespoke mindful activities.

Adult support - heart centre meditation. In this case study it felt important to help Vanessa tune into her son's energy. We did a five-minute heart-centred meditation to identify what James feels and how she could help him. She felt his anxiety and how his 'natural' state was one of nervousness and anxiety. The meditation helped Vanessa see that he responds to her energy. If she isn't calm, he feels this and reflects this back. Vanessa will try to be calmer and more mindful.

I felt that Vanessa's head was full of unending thoughts. I asked her to try a 'mind clearing' meditation each night before going to sleep: imagine a tiny vacuum (or something similar), plugged into the middle of her forehead. It sucks out all the negative and tired thoughts of the day. When it's full or her head is clear, the vacuum rockets up and out into space.

## Mindful activities suggested for James:

Yoga

Vanessa suspects James has poor muscle tone as he frequently complains of tired legs - yoga poses could strengthen his core. I suggested video links appropriate to his age group (see below).

Fish pose - http://tinyurl.com/yoga-fish
Kangaroo - http://tinyurl.com/kangaroo-yoga
Penguin - http://tinyurl.com/penguin-yoga and
    http://tinyurl.com/penguin-yoga2
Polar Bear - http://tinyurl.com/polarbear-yoga and
    http://tinyurl.com/polarbear-yoga2

Meditations

*The golden space suit*; invite your child to imagine he's wearing a special, golden space suit. It has two special qualities: it keeps him safe and shuts out excess noise or energy around him; and it feels like there are really heavy weights in the shoes, so like an astronaut he has to walk more slowly and he feels the weight making a stronger connection to the ground.

This meditation was to help him James's ground and protect his energy; it seemed he was trying to process everything and everyone and it was just too much! To keep him focussed. Vanessa made the meditation physical in that she moved (doing actions) as she guided him with her voice - he pulled on the space suit, but once it was on he closed his eyes and imagined feeling it around his body.

*Fingers and mindfulness bell*; invite him to sit in the chair with his feet on the ground, his eyes closed and the fingertips of both hands touching (thumb to thumb, pinkie to pinkie, etc.) As he listens to the sound of the bell he puts pressure between his thumbs, pushing them together, then releases. On the next breath it's the turn of the index fingers, then the middle fingers and so on until he reaches the pinkies; then he works back to the thumbs.

The mindfulness bell would help change his attention from prolonged sessions in front of his computer screen.

(There is a free mindfulness app on the Insight Timer website - see 'Resources').

Amygdala hold

I suggested that Vanessa apply this mindful technique before bed. It was important that she let his teacher know that the self-hold of the head would be a good calming technique if James was stressed (so he could practise this at nursery).

I encouraged Vanessa to practice regularly (once a day for 3 weeks) even if he wasn't stressed in order that he became accustomed to using it.

Fingertip touch (Varuna mudra)

The mudra (hand position) involves joining the pinkie and thumb on each hand. I felt it would be effective to practise this before and after bedtime, whilst thinking of something that made James happy. Amongst other things, this is known to help with constipation and indigestion problems.

## Feedback (from Vanessa)

*"We are loving the techniques you sent - thank you. I think the golden space suit is a great idea. He really needs it at the moment as he has just started school which is a bit overwhelming for him. It has been perfect timing. He is very anxious so it helps him feel protected.*

*James really likes doing the finger-presses with the mindfulness bell, particularly the pinkie and thumb one (Varuna mudra).*

*I am using the 'mind clearing' meditation at night to try and help my mind relax and I really like it."*

## Conclusions

Sleep was an issue. James used to sleep for 12 hours but was now awake twice each night. He and his family had moved into his grandparents' house (his grandparents recently moved away for 18 months). As James was very close to his grandparents, I suggested that this represented a big change in his life and perhaps he was trying to cope with this emotionally. I was trying to encourage Vanessa to see how adult decisions can affect children; they still feel emotions but don't know how to express them.

Parents usually need a little bit of reflection to realise how children are affected by change. Usually with a gentle guidance they can help children relax.

James was our youngest case study so we had to find ways to engage his interest. There is this myth that younger children can't meditate. I don't believe this to be the case and as the case study demonstrates, patience, repetition and a little bit of imagination can bring positive results.

It was clear that if Vanessa recognised her own stress levels and took gentle steps to bring herself into balance, then her son would feel this and reflect it back.

Through each case study I started to realise the influence the parent's emotions and energy had on the children. In the end, every family I worked with I suggested that the parents practise the mindful breath as this seemed to be very important to the progress we made.

# Matthew, (aged 14) and Mum, Theresa

## Presenting symptoms

Matthew's school and Educational Psychologist defined him as 'presenting as ADHD and Autistic Spectrum'. He has a very limited diet due to sensory issues. In addition he has poor sleep patterns, low energy, co-ordination and concentration difficulties, dyspraxia and poor muscle tone.

He has a poor memory for sequences and constantly loses things, but he can pick up the hidden emotions or tensions in a room very quickly. He finds difficulty in expressing himself or relating a story. He needs instructions to be broken down and explained.

Parent's intention - Theresa's intention for her son, *"Through my own healing journey and experiences with my elder child (diagnosed ADD, on Ritalin etc.) I am aware of the miraculous changes that can happen when simple holistic approaches are used, as well as effort on the part of parents."*

## The Journey...

Heart centre meditation - to help tune into Matthew's energy for insights to create bespoke mindful activities.

Adult support - Theresa was already practising meditation so I encouraged her to trust her intuition when choosing or adapting mindful activities for her son.

## Mindful activities suggested for Matthew:

Yoga

To help Matthew feel more centred and grounded, I suggested Theresa try the yoga posture called Tadasana (mountain pose), trusting her intuition whether to use this before or after the sound meditation practice.

It is one of the simplest poses in yoga as this video demonstrates: http://www.youtube.com/watch?v=ZQKLKwscLVE

Meditations

*Sound meditation*; invite your child to lie on his back and ask him to close his eyes and focus on his breath. Guide him to hear the sound of his breath. Ask him to deliberately make the out-breath (through nose or mouth) louder, like the sound of a wave on the sea; ask him to listen to it and make the sound as long as possible, feeling and hearing this in his ears. After practising this, then invite him to take a silent breath in which he listens and tunes in to the silence. Repeat the 'wave' breaths and silent breaths alternately, so he learns to hear the sound and the silence.

If and when he feels ready, he can replace the 'wave' out-breath with a long sound like 'laaaaa'.

I asked Theresa to practise this with her son every day. I felt it would help to redress the imbalance of ear and throat energy. It would also give him a technique he could focus on when he is in noisy (stressful) situations. Another option is to cover the ears when making the sound as it helps with focus.

Breath and Body; invite your child to lie down on his back with his hands on his chest and to feel the breath in his body (rise and fall of the chest). He could then place his hands on his tummy to feel the breath.

To begin, it is easier to notice the movement of the breath in the body when we are lying down. Noticing the tummy in the breath can encourage the breath to go deeper and it engages the diaphragm to move during the breath (which sends a relaxation signal to the brain).

Hook-ups

I felt that it would be a simple and quick way for Matthew to centre himself when his stress response had been triggered. I encouraged Theresa to form an agreement with Matthew that, when either of started to notice feeling frustrated or stressed, they would do some hook-ups.

This video clip demonstrates the practice and it is scripted in Chapter 14 - 'Developing Emotional Awareness'. https://www.youtube.com/watch?v=3BGWqlEBXxQ

The Mindfulness Bell

Using a mindfulness bell on the computer was to encourage Matthew to practice mindfulness and the breath during day to day activities. When he had noticed a breath, I suggested that he then check his body for tension and let it relax.

The Amygdala Hold

This was to help Matthew move from class to class in school. He had some anger issues and it would help reduce his feelings of rage; practicing this before heading to his next class.

I also suggested that Theresa did the amygdala hold for Matthew - holding his head. During this, the was to think about the word 'calm' - not trying to calm Matthew, but to help her calm her own energy which would influence him.

## Feedback (from Theresa)

*"Having different types of techniques makes it easier for me to choose what resonates with me so that my energy is better focused on helping Matthew.*

*His elder brother sometimes joins us in the meditation. He suggested that we do each breathing technique three times, to enable them both to get into a rhythm or pattern. This is better for all of us, as it enables me to tap into their rhythm and get my voice in sync with their breathing.*

*Matthew and his brother are both completely unwound like uncoiled springs after the above activities. It is early days, but I feel that Matthew is calmer and his posture is a bit better, too. I think there is much more we can do with the breathing and meditation; we can also try focusing on a candle or another object, or using mantras.*

*The mountain yoga pose is very helpful because of what it is supposed to do, but also because it helped me to find out that Matthew finds it very difficult to isolate various muscle groups for tensing and relaxing. He really enjoys doing it.*

*The hook-up is a wonderful technique - we are all doing it now. Initially Matthew found it too difficult to master, but I persevered with showing him the pose and he uses it when he feels stressed.*

*I feel much calmer and more grounded so I will be interested to see how I respond to challenges. Life is much better and many issues have been resolved. On the whole, I would say that children like Matthew benefit from a mixed bag of techniques.*

*We don't use all of the techniques suggested every day, but will either use what Matthew feels like - such as 'hook-up' or mountain pose. I try to continue with focusing on the breath and how he feels in his body, as I believe this is the real route to calmness in the long run.*

*In the past few months, Matthew's appetite has improved and he is trying to eat a more varied diet. He is calmer and less grumpy. He gets anxious about school, but is more amenable and not so focused on words such as 'no' or 'I can't' etc. He has fun with friends in school and is far more independent. His sensory issues are improving and he is learning to dive. He brushes his teeth more thoroughly now and can tolerate a small amount of toothpaste. He has a new mountain bike and hopes to do more cycling to get fit. He feels that his quality of sleep is better too. Looking back over what I originally wrote, it seems like a long time ago. We have all come a long way in a very short time.*

*I forgot to mention that the first part of our collaboration took place when our family was undergoing extremely stressful experiences: traumatic family illness, bereavement, trying to keep a small business going in a difficult climate etc. I know that our situation has improved, but Matthew is normally like a barometer for the family stress. Under the circumstances, he has been extremely calm throughout the whole period. This must be largely due to your input, encouragement and support. Thank you."*

## Conclusion

It was clear that Theresa had been very motivated when trying different mindful activities.

The simple yet effective techniques were focussed on helping Matthew ground his energy and use methods he could easily fit into his routine. Helping him to notice the triggers is a huge step in his awareness as it will help him step in with a mindful activity before it escalates beyond control.

Theresa made a valid point about the power of 'group energy'. If everyone can participate trying the methods you want your children to try, this is much more effective than trying to teach your children while you neglect your own stress levels.

# Working with Special Needs - Catcote Academy (age 14 to 16)

This case study will benefit educators and other professionals as it is a guided approach to developing mindful activities in a professional setting with children and young people.

It was led by Sheila Barnes, one of our Connected Kids tutors with my input and it took place in a professional setting; Catcote Academy in Hartlepool, UK (a secondary, co-educational special school for learners with moderate, severe or profound and multiple learning difficulties). This case study took place with a group of young people aged 14 to 16 whose mental and emotional age was much younger due to their additional support needs.

What is remarkable is that the expectations of these young people and their ability to meditate were initially low; the school staff had their doubts that these young people could focus for any longer than 5 minutes. After regular guided meditation sessions, within a 4 week period, they were able to sit for <u>25 minutes in meditation</u>.

I find this to be truly remarkable and a wakeup call for all of us who think that kids with special needs can't meditate. Yes, they can.

<u>Tutor's intention</u> - The focus was to help the group feel relaxed and introduce them to a number of mindful skills that they could use on a day-to-day basis; these methods would help them manage their feelings and deal with stressful situations.

## The Journey...

The autism co-ordinator, Sarah Houghton-Birrell, assisted Sheila in developing a pilot programme to teach meditation to a small class of pupils with autism.

<u>Preparation</u>

School - Sarah set up a pre-programme session with the teenagers to help them prepare. As visual learners, these teens can be anxious about new experiences. Having read 'Calm Kids', Sarah thought that a mindful activity for the attention span normally suited to 7 - 12 year olds might be the most effective due to their issues with focus and attention.

- The first step was for Sheila to observe the class. Each session would follow the same structure but with a different theme and mindful activity for each session designed to keep them engaged but expand their attention span and sense of relaxation.

- Staff would meet with Sheila to practise some relaxation and become more familiar with the content of each session.

Meditation teacher prep (Sheila)

Heart centre meditation - prior to the session, Sheila practised the heart centre meditation to help her tune in and intuitively develop each session.

*"I meditated while concentrating on each pupil with the intention of receiving ideas on what to cover during my first session. The overriding feeling was to ensure that they concentrated on their breath; this would be the stepping stone to move towards the remaining 3 sessions"*

## Mindful activities for the teen group:

All the sessions involved meditation rather than movement (such as yoga). Each week the tutor, Sheila, intuitively used the results from each session to adapt the content for the following week.

Session 1

Meditation - Feather Breathing

> *Using a colourful feather guide your child to notice it moving as they breathe in and out.*
>
> *After a few breaths, perhaps (with eyes open/closed) gently stroke his face, arms and hands with the feather asking him to notice the sense of touch on his body.*

## Sheila's feedback

*"They loved it and actively stroked their faces and giggled out loud. Noticing this, I invited them to sense that giggle and the feeling in their bodies.*

*I then asked them to place the feather in their cupped hands and continuing to breathe as they imagined that the feather was a tiny baby bird, safe in its nest being gently stroked by their breath. Their focus was amazing. Some chose to close their eyes and some chose to keep their eyes open but they could focus on their breath with greater ease than the members of staff!!"*

Session 2

The teens were invited to remember the 'feather breathing' which they demonstrated easily.

Meditation - fluffy cloud

> *Invite the young person to lie down and imagine he is lying down on a fluffy cloud.*
>
> *He is being lifted up by this cloud and breathing in the feeling of warm sunshine into each part of his body (from the toes and working up) so that he can relax; feeling fluffy and warm as he imagines becoming like the cloud.*

*Guide him to imagine that a gentle wind takes him on a journey, going where he wants to go.*

*Eventually the wind blows him/the cloud back.*

*Then the cloud lowers him gently back to the floor - perhaps using the imagery of a feather floating down from the sky.*

## Sheila's feedback

*"I extended the time from 5 to 10 minutes. I really think that at this stage, 10 minutes is the absolute maximum attention span for these pupils.*

*I also introduced a short sound meditation in the form of " aaahhh" when they were relaxing on the cloud - the closest sound I could get for them that resonated with the heart centre.*

*I considered whether to take along some cotton wool balls so that they could feel them (to help them imagine fluffy clouds) but had decided against it. On reflection I wish I had taken it and given them the option. This group really like sensory work, particularly the sense of touch."*

Session 3

Sheila had persuaded the school to give her a 1-hour session with the teens. She made arrangements for the technician to project an underwater scene onto the walls and she used some shells for them to choose and use as part of the meditation.

Meditation - shell

*Guide your child to sit on the floor and explain that you are going to use some shells as the theme for the meditation is the sea.*

*Bring in the awareness of breath as you did in the 'feather breathing' session (this time noticing the breath without the*

236

*feather but using the memory/imagination of this to support awareness of the breath).*

*Help him to focus on the shell with mindful awareness; noticing the patterns, feeling the 'bumpy' side and the smooth side.*

*Invite him to lie down on the floor holding the shell and imagine that he is the shell lying on the sea floor - safe and warm.*

*Invite him to imagine that the water is like a warm bath warming his toes, legs and helping his tummy feel 'smiley' inside.*

*When he notices that feeling, he can rub the side of the shell which is his favourite side.*

*Now invite him to imagine coloured fish all around as you count to five - he can have different fish (shape and size) and different colours (favourite colour).*

*Continue to invite him to relax with each out breath as he notices the fish.*

*You could guide him to imagine he is the colour of his favourite fish.*

*Finally, guide him back to his breath and his body but still aware of the nice feeling in his tummy when he strokes the shell.*

## Sheila's feedback

*"The meditation lasted about 20 minutes (including the time spent looking at the shells). They had managed to imagine their own coloured fish and felt relaxed. We had a little chat and then I explained that they could draw a picture of their fish and their meditation. I played some whale music and encouraged them to continue with the 'feather breathing' while they drew their pictures.*

*I felt it was important to build on the meditation themes, from the 'feather breathing' to the feeling of floating and relaxation and the sensation of touch.*

*Moving forward I feel that the meditation should develop into a journey on a boat with the 'feather breathing' blowing the sails to make the boat move, seeing the fluffy clouds in the sky and perhaps making it a glass bottomed boat so that they can imagine seeing underwater.*

*I also chose to develop a picture of this meditation so that they can attach the tactile items we have used; the feather on a bird, the cotton wool for a cloud, the shell in the ocean and eventually some silk squares for the sail of their boat. There will be a flag on the top of the boat so that they can add their name. This will leave them with a collage of tactile items and a reminder of the meditations; they can then use them as and when they want to and the staff could implement them into their work too.*

*It feels right to build on each session's storyline and use similar guidelines so that they are more familiar with what to do and can relax more easily with each session."*

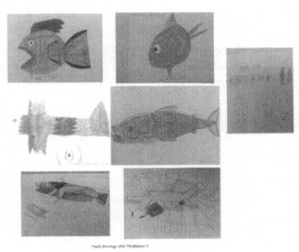

*Credit: Sheila Barnes*

## Session 4

The group had been advised that this was the last session and apparently they were very sad.

Meditation - sailing ship

> *Guide your child to relax using the 'feather breathing' and any other words to help him relax his body.*
>
> *Now ask your child to imagine that he is on a beautiful ship; an old one such as a galleon, of which he is the captain.*
>
> *Ask him to imagine the birds and their soft feathers flying in the sky, the clouds drifting slowly through the blue sky, the warm sea with its colourful fish and shells and the wind blowing the colourful sails to take him gently forward on his journey.*
>
> *Ask him to imagine what it feels like to have the sense of freedom and space on the sea, the sense of happiness (or whatever he is feeling) in his body.*
>
> *Use mindfulness to guide him through the different sensations and feelings that come up.*

## Sheila's feedback

*"This was probably the longest meditation we had completed - 25 minutes.*

*Afterwards I gave each young person the picture and the components; with each one they were reminded of what they had practised (the feather breath, blowing the sail and the cloud).*

*They absolutely loved the physical reminders of their work and all said that they would put them in their personal trays and use them. The teacher asked when, where and how they would use what they had learned. Some replied "at school", "at home" and some said while "walking with their dog.*

*All of the elements I used were based on those things that they have access to on a daily basis and which were tangible. The overriding theme throughout was the 'feather breath' which they immediately understood. This was used as an aid to help focus on the breath due to the movement of the feather. The tactile nature of the feather brought in the sense of touch (brushing across the face, arms and hands) to help bring in a connection and awareness to the body.*

*I am so glad I followed my intuition and didn't hold myself back with the limited expectations suggested by staff. Week by week the group proved that they were capable of so much more. Who was really teaching who? We started off slowly and then built a longer and longer session, reiterating and building upon each element. I wish I could work with their parents/carers, I know it would help them too."*

## School's feedback (Sarah)

*"From the staff we gathered that the pilot group found the specific sessions, relaxing, enjoyable and interesting and the sessions gave them a useful, possibly vital, life tool. Their weekly evaluations were consistently good to excellent.*

*Since the session the ideas have been used on a day to day basis in the group as required and some of our young people have used the techniques at home. Our next steps as a school are to provide staff, and in time parents, with an awareness of the principals and then move onto training them so that they begin to integrate the techniques into everyday life in school and give as many of our young people as possible the benefits our pilot group gained."*

*Credit: Sheila Barnes*

## Conclusion

The use of the breath in a tactile, mindful way was an excellent way to help these young people have a focus. When we teach anyone meditation, the breath is a key point as it is the anchor in every moment. Giving these teens a way to do this became a foundation block for the remainder sessions.

Once they had worked with the breath, this enabled them to connect to (and relax) their bodies. Without feeling relaxed, meditation can be very challenging for any beginner. Working with the body and helping them to relax was a way to combine the focus of the breath into the body and help it de-stress through relaxation. When we are relaxed, we can learn.

For the final sessions, the use of objects that reflected the imagery for the guided meditations was an excellent way for these teens to learn and process this meditation 'story' in a way that matched their abilities. I truly believe that these children are teaching us how to adapt the way we meditate as many adults can become restricted by what they believe meditation should be and whether or not children (especially those with special needs) can meditate.

## Managing Chronic Pain with Meditation

This following information didn't come from one of our case studies, but it was a session that a Connected Kids Tutors ran and I felt it demonstrated the power of teaching children meditation when they experience chronic pain.

*I was invited to teach a restorative yoga class during the evening educational segment at a local camp. It was a group of 50 children ranging from 9-16 years who cope with chronic pain due to arthritis, autoimmune disease, and Ehlers-Danlos Syndrome.*

*When I spoke to the camp organizer, it was clear to me that the children needed mindful experiences to have a sense of control and well-being in their bodies - it's so easy to want to ignore a body when in chronic pain.*

*I had 50 minutes to make it happen for a room of 50 kids.*

*When the children entered, aside from one child in a wheelchair and one that insisted her body could not move, it was like any room full of children; active, vibrant and a little hard to contain. I divided the group into 4 pods by laying out sections of yoga mats and having them form a circle on that set of mats. I've learned in my years of work with children that their energy expands into the space they're given, and large room and large group equals large energy. The pods created smaller spaces, and the energy immediately shifted.*

*I invited them to do some opening movement to get into their bodies (similar to the Phoenix Rising Yoga Therapy approach that I am trained in) that matched their energy level. Again there was another shift of energy in the room. They were in their bodies, and now I had their attention.*

*I taught them about their brains and I had them try a couple postures and notice what came up for them in their minds and bodies. I laughed with the goofiness that simply must emerge when a group of children comes together and invited them back into their experience. In this way, I provided permission to be a kid and met them where they were. I am aware that by flowing with the kids, I am teaching mindfulness by example—not judging the current moment but acknowledging it. I stayed authentically with them and would guide them back into their experience simply by asking questions that guided them back to the moment.*

*They learned about their breath. They experienced their bodies. Then I did something bold: I invited them to notice a part that felt closed or tight or pained.*

*With gentle guidance, I asked them to do it if it felt safe, just as an experiment. We turned the sensation up and we turned it down and noticed what happened. I invited them to find the opposite experience in their body and I asked them to share.*

*A couple of kids reported feeling more relaxed. I asked them what it felt like. Then one girl got brave and shared, "What if all it is is pain?" She expressed feeling trapped in her body. I could feel the room squirm a little. I looked at her and reflected it back. I told her it was okay and that she didn't have to feel anything other than what she was feeling. I could sense her self-expectations soften. She then shared that she could feel the subtle shifts up and down in sensation. All she needed was a witness that accepted whatever the answer was; being seen and witnessed in a non-judging way allowed her to do that for herself.*

*After some fun partner poses to match a resurgence in energy, I guided a 20 minute relaxation; fifty children with only two wiggling and giggling. I placed my hands on the soles of the wigglers' feet, and their energy settled and magic happened. They tuned in and everyone suddenly had permission to not be a performer for others but to simply be.*

*At the end, the girl who felt only pain asked for a recording of what we did together. She found something that she didn't even know she was seeking!"*

Renee Proctor Groenemann, Spirited Growth

# EPILOGUE

## March 2013

## Connections

10 years ago, I was just starting my journey of teaching meditation and practising healing therapies.

Before starting this new 'career', I was on holiday in the Isle of Skye and happened to hear a radio programme about a man who'd had autism as a child. I say *had* autism as he was 'cured' by his parents, who developed the Son-Rise Programme (which is a programme in the USA designed to help parents/educators engage with their children on the spectrum). They had been advised to place him into an institution, but they decided to try and help him.

I recall him saying: *"They entered my world and brought me into theirs."* Those words have stayed with me ever since.

Perhaps those words were the inspirational drive that has led me to write 2 books about teaching meditation. To me, it seems quite profound.

## More connections

To get the peace and quiet to write this second book, we hired a cottage in Skye and prior to our arrival a friend gave me a crystal. I recognised it immediately as a blue lace agate: this crystal works with the throat chakra, the energy centre in the body that links to communication. It was the perfect gift!

On the first night I found I couldn't sleep, so I decided to read a book called 'Crystals and Sacred Sites' by Judy Hall. I flicked through it and found myself reading about the crystal. There was a prayer/invocation at the end and I thought it was so appropriate I have included it here.

There have many experiences like this in my life, like little hints from the universe. I'm no stranger to all these 'connections' - in fact, this is how my first book was written. Every day I am amazed at these 'connections'. I thank God/Source for these little treasures that are presented to me, letting me know that I'm on the right path, heading in the right direction and fulfilling my purpose.

My first book, 'Calm Kids', seemed easier to write because I had been teaching children meditation and the 'Connected Kids' programme which teaches other adults to do the same. I was simply re-calling my experiences and presenting them in a practical way.

But this book is different. It was written from the heart.

### The Prayer of Saint Francis (variation)

*Lord, make me an instrument of thy peace.*
*Where there is hatred, let me sow love;*
*Where there is injury, pardon;*
*Where there is doubt, faith;*
*Where there is despair, hope;*
*Where there is darkness, light;*
*Where there is sadness, joy.*
*Let peace remain in my heart and throughout the world.*

I decided to re-write the 2nd book before it was released as a paperback (given that it would be in print forever!) I had learned so much more that I wanted to share and every moment is a new moment to learn - it never, ever ends.

# ACKNOWLEDGEMENTS

Producing this book has been an incredible journey. I am fortunate to know Jo Woolf who helped me take my ramblings and edit them into a book. Thanks are also due to Sian Graham who designed this wonderful book cover.

I am grateful to the contributors who kindly agreed to the inclusion of their material and we have listed them in our resources section so you can follow up their amazing work.

A special thanks goes to the many lovely people I know and who kindly gave me their time, encouragement and contributions

Lesley Brannen, Liz Bell, Christine Curtis-Perez, Heather Mackenzie, Liz Devine, Andrea Duffin, Sheila Barnes, Sarah Houghton-Birrel, Gillian Duncan, Pam Jeffs, Lorraine Cameron, Mandy Singh, Clare Gibbons, Elizabeth Laird, Linsey Denham, Jane Burgess, Dodi Mitchell, Laura Mirante, Dee Taylor, Charlene Scott, Karen Harris, Ashley Watson, Audrey Hird, Jen Baxter, Hazel Melia, Nic Foxe, Suzi Gibson, Helen Monaghan, Angela Connolly, Kimberly Snider Sterrs, Hollie Neal, Kay Locke, Helen Harris, Julie Woolrich-Moon, Alisoun Mackenzie, Anna Kovacks, Deborah Dalziel, Karen Davies, Jude Brown, Helen Jacoby, Bridget Mary-Clare, Renee Proctor Groenemann, Beth Studdiford and Avril McGill.

I am so lucky to have a wonderful husband, Bruce, who never complains about the hours I spend away with work or writing and I feel truly blessed (thanks for all the cups of tea). My family of Jess (our black lab) and our pussycats Siouxsie and Sam help me to practise mindfulness with their waggy tails and purrs of joy.

I have a special shout out to everyone who has followed my campaign on social media to raise awareness of teaching children meditation and who so willingly share this information (and plant seeds of ideas all over the world!)

I have had some wonderful teachers in my time, Kim McManus, Andrew and Frieda Bacon (who taught me that the most important words in the English language were 'thank you') and also Thich Nhat Hanh, Jonathan Goldman, Dr Emoto and Donna Eden who have all inspired me with their work.

My own journey through childhood has been a challenging one though I am grateful for all the experiences of life and realising that my mum and dad both struggled with the challenge of mental health; meditation saved my mum but it was too late for my father. Had they been taught mindfulness as kids, their lives could have been so different.

I couldn't have taken this forward without all the families who gave up their time to try the techniques and suggestions I made - my heartfelt thanks to you all.

Finally, a special note of gratitude to all the children I have met, heard about or spoken to who are viewed by this world as being 'autistic'. Thank you for being my greatest teachers.

# RESOURCES

*A list of useful sources, tools, toys and ideas that have helped autistic children or those with ADHD or other special needs, as well as the people who care for them.*

## WEBSITES

**Teach Children Meditation** - www.teachchildrenmeditation.com (Connected Kids courses, meditation cds and products)

**Jonathan Goldman** - **www.healingsounds.com**

**Di Williams, 'Still Paths'** - **www.diwilliams.com**

**Emoto peace project for children** - **www.emotoproject.com/english/picturebook.html**

**Alltogetherkids** - www.alltogetherkids.co.uk (specialises in baby support)

**Mandalas** - **www.art-is-fun.com**

**Masaru Emoto's experiments with ice crystals** - **www.masaru-emoto.net**

**Tuning forks and healing** - **www.re-creationfoundation.com**

**Plum village monastery** - plumvillage.org (Thich Nhat Hanh retreat)

**Liz Bell** - lizrbell@talktalk.net (mandalas and crystals)

**Lesley Brannen** - **lesley.brannen@lineone.net** (mandalas)

**Yoga and Mudra poses** - Hollie Neal - **www.littleyogischool.com**

Andrea Duffin - www.facebook.com/pages/The-YOGA-Forest/604183502953019

Jennifer Robinson - Breatheasy kids breatheasykids@gmail.com (amygdala hold)

Kay Locke - www.facebook.com/kay.locke2

Helen Harris - www.reflexology-polarity.co.uk/ (facial massage)

Nicola Foxe - www.yo-yoyoga.ie (mandala picture)

Linsey Denham - bachflowerconsultsonline.publishpath.com

Dodi Mitchell - infinitesoulshealing.com/

Kimberly Snider Sterrs - www.facebook.com/meditatingyouthheartsconnect

Julie Woolrich-Moon - http://www.facebook.com/hushawhile

Karen Davies - www.conversationswithabutterfly.com/

Sheila Barnes - www.eternal-circle.co.uk/ (group case study)

Renee Proctor Groenemann - www.facebook.com/spiritedgrowth (case study)

Deborah Dalziel - www.melbournereikicentre.com.au

www.nationalautismresources.com

www.autismresearchcentre.com

East Chesire Autism Parents Support - www.space4autism.com/

Free meditations for young people - smilingmind.com.au/

Energy Medicine - Donna Eden - innersource.net/em/

## VIDEOS

**Hook ups - http://tinyurl.com/hookup-DE**

**Yoga poses**

**Fish pose -http://tinyurl.com/yoga-fish**

**Kangaroo - http://tinyurl.com/kangaroo-yoga**

**Penguin - http://tinyurl.com/penguin-yoga and http://tinyurl.com/penguin-yoga2**

**Polar Bear - http://tinyurl.com/polarbear-yoga and http://tinyurl.com/polarbear-yoga2**

**Spanish - http://tinyurl.com/yoga-kids-spanish**

**Mindful breathing - kids**

**Spanish - http://tinyurl.com/mindful-breath-spanish-kids**

**English -http://tinyurl.com/mindful-breath-english-kids**

**Energy Medicine - Donna Eden - http://tinyurl.com/energy-donnaeden**

## BOOKS

*'Calm Kids: Help Children Relax with Mindful Activities'* by Lorraine Murray, Floris Books, 2012

*'Healing Sounds: The Power of Harmonics'* by Jonathan Goldman, pub. Healing Arts Press, 2002

*'How to Talk So Kids Will Listen and Listen So Kids Will Talk'* by Adele Faber and Elaine Mazlish, pub. Piccadilly Press, 2013

'*It's the Thought that Counts: Why Mind Over Matter Really Works'* by Dr David Hamilton, pub. Hay House, 2008

'*Labyrinth - Landscape of the Soul'* by Di Williams, pub. Wild Goose Publications, Glasgow, 2011

'*Mudras - Yoga in your Hands'* by Gertrud Hirschi, pub. Red Wheel/Weiser, 2000

'*Planting Seeds with Music and Songs: Practising Mindfulness with Children'* by Thich Nhat Hanh, Chan Chau Nghiem & Wietske Vriezen, pub. Parallax Press, 2013

'*Smart Moves: Why Learning Is Not All In Your Head'* by Carla Hannaford, pub. Great Ocean Publishers, 2005

'*The 7 Secrets of Sound Healing'* by Jonathan Goldman, pub. Hay House, 2008

'*The Emotional Life of Your Brain'* by Sharon Begley and Richard Davidson, pub. Hodder, 2012

'*The Hidden Messages in Water'* by Masaru Emoto, pub. Atria Books, 2011

'*Tickle Your Amygdala'* by Neil Slade, Kindle edition, 2012

'*Water Crystal Healing: Music and Images to Restore your Well-Being'* by Masaru Emoto, pub. Atria Books, 2012

'*Working with the Labyrinth: Paths for Exploration'* Ruth Sewell, Jan Sellers and Di Williams, pub. Wild Goose Publications, Glasgow, 2013

'*Yoga Pretzels: 50 Fun Yoga Activities for Kids and Grownups'* (Yoga Cards) by Tara Guber, pub. Barefoot Books Ltd, 2005

'*Awakening Joy: 10 Steps to True Happiness'* by James Baraz and

Shoshana Alexander, Parallax Press 2013

*'Emotional Intelligence: Why it Can Matter More Than IQ'* by Daniel Goleman, pub. Bloomsbury Publishing PLC, 1996

*'Labyrinths Meditative Coloring Book'* by artist/author Aliyah Schick, Sacred Imprints 2011

*'The Psoas Book'* by Liz Koch, Atlantic Books; 2 Rev Exp edition 1998 www.coreawareness.com/categories/products

*'The Awakening Child'* by Heather Mackenzie, to be published in 2016

*'I am Henry Finch'* by Alexis Deacon, Walker Books, Jan. 2015

## TOOLS, TOYS AND GAMES

**Mediation Apps - www.braininhand.co.uk, www.headspace.com/headspace-meditation-app, touchautism.com, insighttimer.com**

**Weighted blankets - www.weight2goblankets.co.uk, www.sensorygoods.com**

**'Fidget toys' - http://www.specialneedstoys.com/uk/**

**Problem-solving - http://autismteachingstrategies.com/free-social-skills-downloads-2/**

**Emotion response cards from Where Dragons Fly - www.wheredragonsfly.net/shop.htm**

**Pink and green - soft toys for meditation - www.etsy.com/UK/shop/PinkGreenCrochet**

**Pilgrim Paths - tactile labyrinths - http://www.pilgrimpaths.co.uk**

## Articles/Research

### Chapter 2

'Earthing: Health Implications of Reconnecting the Human Body to the Earth's Surface Electrons' Gaétan Chevalier, Stephen T. Sinatra, James L. Oschman, Karol Sokal and Pawel Sokal - Journal of Environmental Public Health. Volume 2012 (2012) - http://tinyurl.com/earthing-ck

### Chapter 4

'What you should know about your brain' *by Dr Judy Willis* - http://tinyurl.com/brain-ck

'Meditation That Eases Anxiety? Brain Scans Show Us How' - http://tinyurl.com/brainscan-ck

'Only 25 Minutes of Mindfulness Meditation Alleviates Stress, According to Carnegie Mellon Researchers', Carnegie Mellon University, Pittsburgh, July 2014 - http://tinyurl.com/carnegie-ck

'TM Chills out a High School', Newhaven Independent, April 2014 - http://tinyurl.com/newhaven-ck

'Meditation experience is associated with differences in default mode network activity and connectivity' - http://tinyurl.com/connect-ck

'Meditation experience is associated with increased cortical thickness' - http://tinyurl.com/cortical-ck

'Meditation really works' - http://tinyurl.com/meditationworks-ck

'Mediation strengthens the brain' - http://tinyurl.com/brain-strength-ck

'Meditation's positive residual effects', 'Turn down the volume', 'Eight weeks to a better brain' - http://tinyurl.com/positive-ck

'Oxytocin enhances brain function in children with autism' - http://tinyurl.com/oxytocin-autism-ck

'Increased dopamine tone during meditation-induced change of consciousness' - http://tinyurl.com/dopamine-ck

'It's the Thought that Counts: Why Mind Over Matter Really Works' *by Dr David Hamilton, pub. Hay House, 2008* - www.hayhouse.co.uk


Chapter 6

Heart Math Institute - tinyurl.com/heartmath-ck


Chapter 9

www.masaru-emoto.net


Chapter 10

'Limiting Aggression through self control' - http://tinyurl.com/aggression-ck


Chapter 11

Labyrinths - wooden and cloth versions - www.pilgrimpaths.co.uk

## Chapter 12

'Excessive Stress Disrupts the Architecture of the Developing Brain' - Jan 2014 - http://tinyurl.com/harvard-ck

'Amygdala and autism's checkered history' - tinyurl.com/amyg-ck

'The Psoas Muscle' - www.coreawareness.com

## Chapter 13

Kay Locke - www.space4autism.com

**More useful articles on Autism, ADHD and mindful activities**

**The effects of yoga on the attention and behavior of boys with Attention-Deficit/hyperactivity Disorder (ADHD)** - Jensen PS, Kenny DT. J Atten Disord. 2004 May;7(4):205-16 - http://tinyurl.com/yoga-autism

**Application of integrated yoga therapy to increase imitation skills in children with autism spectrum disorder** - Radhakrishna S, Int J Yoga. 2010 Jan;3(1):26-30 - **http://tinyurl.com/autism-yoga2**

**Efficacy of the Get Ready to Learn yoga program among children with autism spectrum disorders: a pretest-posttest control group design** - Koenig KP, Buckley-Reen A, Garg S. Am J Occup Ther. 2012 Sep;66(5):538-46 - **http://tinyurl.com/autism-yoga3**

**Relaxation response-based yoga improves functioning in young children with autism: a pilot study** - Rosenblatt LE, Gorantla S, Torres JA, Et al J Altern Complement Med. 2011 Nov;17(11):1029-35 - http://tinyurl.com/autism-yoga4

Exercise is ADHD Medication - http://tinyurl.com/exercise-adhd-medicatino

Helping kids to access emotions - http://tinyurl.com/kids-emotions

Mindful eating plate - http://tinyurl.com/meditation-food

Emotional intelligence - http://tinyurl.com/emotion-int

Anxiety in Kids - www.heysigmund.com/anxiety-in-kids/

10 Tools for students to fidget in the classroom - http://tinyurl.com/mind-fidget

Made in the USA
San Bernardino, CA
04 December 2018